THE CARTOON GUIDE TO
THE COMPUTER

Also by Larry Gonick

The Cartoon History of the Universe
The Cartoon Guide to Physics (with Art Huffman)
The Cartoon Guide to the Computer
The Cartoon Guide to Genetics (with Mark Wheelis)

THE CARTOON GUIDE TO
COMPUTER

LARRY GONICK

HarperPerennial

A Division of HarperCollins*Publishers*

FIRST HARPERPERENNIAL edition published 1991

The Library of Congress has cataloged the previous edition of this book as follows:

Gonick, Larry.
  The cartoon guide to computer science.

  (College outline series; CO/417)
  Includes index.
  Summary: An introduction to computer science in cartoon format.
  1. Computers—Caricatures and cartoons. 2. Electronic data processing—Caricatures and cartoons. [1. Computers—Cartoons and comics. 2. Data processing—Cartoons and comics. 3. Cartoons and comics] I. Title. II. Series.
QA76.G593   1983   001.64   82-48251
ISBN 0-06-460417-9 (pbk.)

ISBN 0-06-273097-5 (pbk.)

91 92 93 94 95 RRD 10 9 8 7 6 5 4 3 2 1

CONTENTS

PART I
THE AGES OF INFORMATION

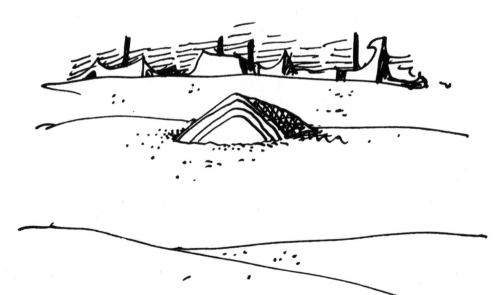

CLEARLY, THE AGE DEMANDS A PIECE OF TECHNOLOGY SOLELY DEVOTED TO STORING, CLASSIFYING, SORTING, COMPARING, COMBINING, AND DISPLAYING INFORMATION AT HIGH SPEED!

THAT, AND A SHOVEL...

THAT PIECE OF EQUIPMENT IS THE **COMPUTER**.

THIS EXPLAINS WHY COMPUTERS ARE POPPING UP WHEREVER INFORMATION COUNTS, FROM THE BIGGEST BUSINESSES TO THE LITTLEST WRISTWATCH!

IT'S ENOUGH TO MAKE YOU PARANOID!

AND IT ALSO ACCOUNTS FOR THE FACT THAT BEFORE YOU CAN UNDERSTAND COMPUTERS, IT HELPS TO KNOW SOMETHING ABOUT INFORMATION FIRST— SUCH AS, FOR EXAMPLE, WHAT IT IS...

WHAT IS IT? IT'S... IT'S... AH... UM... ER... WHAT A STUPID QUESTION!

What is information?

IN THE EVERYDAY SENSE OF THE WORD, "INFORMATION" MEANS *FACTS*: THE SORT OF STUFF THAT FILLS NON FICTION BOOKS, AND CAN ONLY BE EXPRESSED IN WORDS.

IN THE WORLD OF COMPUTERS, HOWEVER, THE TERM HAS A MUCH BROADER MEANING.

THE MODERN DEFINITION COMES FROM **CLAUDE SHANNON**, A BELL LABS ENGINEER, AMATEUR UNICYCLIST, AND FOUNDER OF THE SCIENCE OF *INFORMATION THEORY.*

MEEP!

SHANNON ALSO BUILT AN ELECTRIC "MOUSE" THAT COULD BE PROGRAMMED TO RUN MAZES!

7

ACCORDING TO SHANNON, INFORMATION IS PRESENT WHENEVER A SIGNAL IS TRANSMITTED FROM ONE PLACE TO ANOTHER:

IT DOESN'T MATTER WHAT KIND OF SIGNAL IT IS. FOR EXAMPLE:

THE SIGNAL MAY BE IN THE FORM OF **WORDS**, THE MOST FAMILIAR KIND OF INFORMATION...

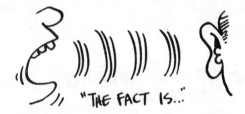

"THE FACT IS..."

...BUT A *PICTURE* ALSO SENDS A SIGNAL, IN THE FORM OF LIGHT WAVES, TO OUR EYES. IT LOOKS AS IF PICTURES CONVEY INFORMATION!

FURTHERMORE, OUR EYE SENDS A PATTERN OF ELECTRIC IMPULSES UP THE OPTIC NERVE TO THE BRAIN. THAT SIGNAL CARRIES INFORMATION, TOO!!

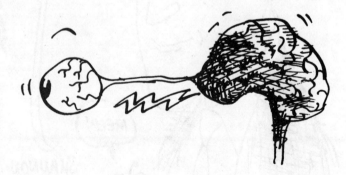

MUSIC IS A SIGNAL OF SORTS, CONVEYING INFORMATION IMPOSSIBLE TO PUT INTO WORDS...

FOR THAT MATTER, A *PUNCH IN THE MOUTH* IS NOT WITHOUT ITS INFORMATION VALUE!

GET THE MESSAGE?

SO YOU SEE... INFORMATION COMES IN MANY FORMS: VERBAL, VISUAL, MUSICAL, ETC, ETC ETC... ALL OF WHICH CAN BE HANDLED BY COMPUTERS. WHY, A COMPUTER CAN DELIVER A *HYDROGEN BOMB*, NOT JUST A *PUNCH IN THE MOUTH*!!

DO YOU THINK THEY'RE TRYING TO TELL US SOMETHING??

9

ALL THOSE SIGNALS, INCLUDING A PUNCH IN THE MOUTH, CAN BE RECORDED IN SOME WAY... SUGGESTING THAT INFORMATION CAN BE *STORED* AS WELL AS TRANSMITTED AND RECEIVED...

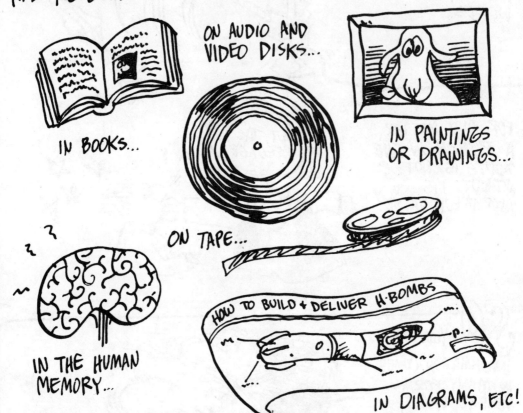

IN BOOKS...

ON AUDIO AND VIDEO DISKS...

IN PAINTINGS OR DRAWINGS...

ON TAPE...

IN THE HUMAN MEMORY...

HOW TO BUILD & DELIVER H-BOMBS

IN DIAGRAMS, ETC!

THE POINT OF THIS IS TO TRANSMIT THE SAME MESSAGE MANY TIMES...

AH!

AND OF COURSE, ITEMS OF INFORMATION CAN BE COMBINED IN VARIOUS WAYS.

AS IN ONE PLUS ONE!

MEEP MEEP!

AND YOU CAN **VERB** ANY WORD IN THE LANGUAGE!

WE REFER TO THE STORAGE, TRANSMISSION, COMBINATION, AND COMPARISON OF MESSAGES AS

INFORMATION PROCESSING.

(ALTHOUGH THE COMPUTER INDUSTRY IS GUILTY OF TURNING MANY NOUNS INTO VERBS — ACCESS, INPUT, INTERFACE — "PROCESS" WAS ALREADY A VERB, THANKS TO THE FOOD BUSINESS...)

PROCESSED CHEESE

PROCESSED HAM

PROCESSED INFORMATION

TO APPRECIATE THE POWER OF INFORMATION, CONSIDER ANOTHER EVERYDAY EXAMPLE:

LIFE ITSELF.

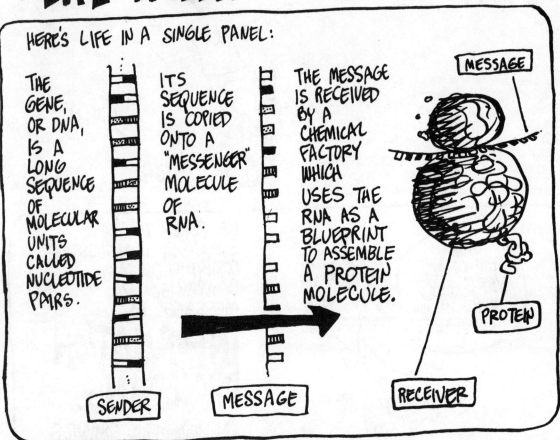

HERE'S LIFE IN A SINGLE PANEL:

THE GENE, OR DNA, IS A LONG SEQUENCE OF MOLECULAR UNITS CALLED NUCLEOTIDE PAIRS.

SENDER

ITS SEQUENCE IS COPIED ONTO A "MESSENGER" MOLECULE OF RNA.

MESSAGE

THE MESSAGE IS RECEIVED BY A CHEMICAL FACTORY WHICH USES THE RNA AS A BLUEPRINT TO ASSEMBLE A PROTEIN MOLECULE.

MESSAGE

PROTEIN

RECEIVER

IN OTHER WORDS, THE PROTEIN IS BUILT ACCORDING TO **INFORMATION** STORED IN THE GENE.

FOR DETAILS, SEE THE CARTOON GUIDE TO GENETICS!

THE TRICK IS THIS: CERTAIN PROTEINS HELP DNA TO **REPRODUCE**.

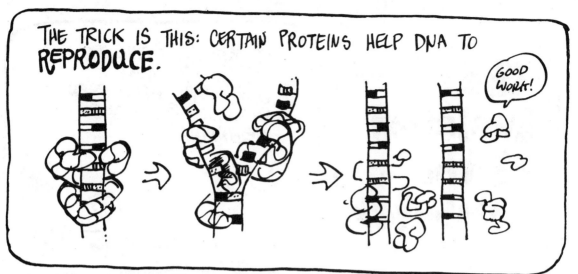

WHAT HAPPENS THEN? IF DNA ENCODES PROTEINS THAT HELP DNA TO REPRODUCE, THEN MORE OF THOSE PROTEINS WILL BE BUILT, MORE DNA WILL BE COPIED...ETC! MOREOVER, IF THE DNA ENCODES OTHER PROTEINS WHICH PROTECT IT IN VARIOUS WAYS, AND OTHERS TO ATTACK AND DESTROY RIVAL DNA AND PROTEINS...

THEN THAT DNA-PROTEIN SYSTEM WILL REPRODUCE ITSELF AGAIN AND AGAIN — AND THAT'S WHAT YOU CALL A **LIFE FORM**.

SO LIFE ITSELF IS A MOLECULAR INFORMATION PROCESSOR, WHICH HAS BEEN RUNNING AUTOMATICALLY FOR OVER **3 BILLION YEARS !!**

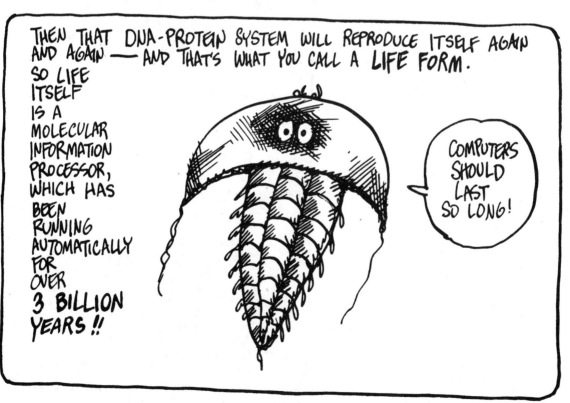

The Evolution of the Computer

IT MAY BE GOING TOO FAR TO SAY THAT COMPUTERS HAVE BEEN EVOLVING FROM THE BEGINNING...

BUT FROM EARLY TIMES, LIFE FORMS HAVE BEEN INCREASING THEIR INFORMATION-PROCESSING ABILITIES. EVEN AN AMOEBA RECEIVES CHEMICAL SIGNALS TELLING IT WHERE THE FOOD IS!

OTHERWISE, I'D HAVE TO EAT EVERYTHING!

14

ALL THE **SENSES** ARE WAYS OF RECEIVING SIGNALS:

BUT THEN WE CALL IT PURR-CEIVING!

THE EYES PERCEIVE A RANGE OF ELECTROMAGNETIC RAYS; THE EARS RESPOND TO PRESSURE IN THE AIR; THE NOSE REACTS TO VARIOUS MOLECULES; SO DO THE TASTE BUDS; AND THE SENSE OF TOUCH IS A WAY OF RECEIVING A PUNCH IN THE MOUTH!

SENSORY IMPRESSIONS ARE TRANSMITTED ELECTRICALLY ALONG THE NERVES AND COORDINATED BY THE BRAIN — NATURE'S FIRST ATTEMPT TO BUILD A COMPUTER!!

HM! ROTTEN RESPONSE TIME!

THESE "MICROS" ARE SLOW!

BESIDES TRANSMITTING INFORMATION WITHIN THEIR OWN BODIES, ANIMALS ALSO SENT MESSAGES TO EACH OTHER:

GRONK

NOTE AGAIN: THESE DO NOT NECESSARILY CONVEY INFORMATION THAT CAN BE EXPRESSED IN WORDS!

WHAT DO YOU MEAN, WHAT DOES "GRONK" MEAN? "GRONK" MEANS "GRONK!"

ANYWAY— WHAT DOES "MEAN" MEAN?

ALSO:

THESE MESSAGES ARE NOT ALWAYS IN THE FORM OF SOUNDS. DOGS COMMUNICATE BY WAGGING THEIR TAILS, AND BEES CAN DESCRIBE THE PRECISE LOCATION OF A FLOWER BY "DANCING."

I DON'T THINK WE'RE SPEAKING THE SAME LANGUAGE...

WHEN HUMANS BEGAN COMMUNICATING, THEY PROBABLY WEREN'T MUCH DIFFERENT FROM ANY OTHER ANIMAL.

"GRONK"

"GRONK.."

GRONK

GRONK

BUT AS THE BRAIN INCREASED IN SIZE AND "COMPUTING POWER," LANGUAGE BECAME MORE EXPRESSIVE.

The reason?

PEOPLE COULD REMEMBER AND USE MORE WORDS. THE MORE WORDS THEY USED, THE GREATER THE NUMBER OF POSSIBLE MESSAGES — WHICH IS ANOTHER WAY OF SAYING THEY COULD SEND MORE INFORMATION.

THE SKY IS BLUE...

THE SKY IS BLUE AND FLECKED WITH CLOUDS...

THE SKY, CLEARING AFTER YESTERDAY'S RAIN, IS BLUE AND FLECKED WITH CLOUDS.

GRONK

ALONG WITH WORDS CAME THE RULES FOR COMBINING WORDS: THE LAWS OF **GRAMMAR** AND **LOGIC.**

IF YOU COME OUT **AND** APOLOGIZE, **THEN** WE WILL **NOT** FLAY YOU ALIVE, **UNLESS** WE CHANGE OUR MINDS...

IN TIME, HOWEVER, IT APPEARED THERE WAS A SPECIAL TYPE OF WORD WITH ITS OWN SPECIAL RULES... NAMELY —

WAIT **ONE** MINUTE... LET GUESS...

NUMBERS

YOU CAN COUNT ON THEM!

NUMBERS ARE PRECISE... RELIABLE... YOU CAN ADD, SUBTRACT AND MULTIPLY NUMBERS... "ONE PLUS ONE" MAKES SENSE, BUT AS THEY SAY, YOU CAN'T ADD GRAPES AND REINDEER.

EXCEPT IN MY GRAPE AND REINDEER STEW....

18

NUMBERS ARE ALSO UNIQUE IN THAT YOU "DO THEM" ON YOUR FINGERS, WHILE OTHER PARTS OF LANGUAGE HAPPEN MAINLY IN YOUR HEAD... YES, COUNTING HAS BEEN **DIGITAL*** FROM THE BEGINNING!

HOW MANY DAYS IN A MONTH?

SIMPLE! ONE, TWO, THREE, FOUR, FIVE, SIX, SEVEN, EIGHT, NINE...

TEN...

...

AHEM! WHILE I'M SURE THIS QUESTION *HAS* AN ANSWER, THE CURRENT GENERATION OF *HARDWARE* SEEMS INADEQUATE TO THE TASK...

I SAY!

THESE GENIUSES CERTAINLY CAN STRAIN THE OLD SOCIAL FABRIC...

NINETEEN...

* "DIGIT" MEANS FINGER!

NOW, HAVING COUNTED, WAS THERE SOME WAY TO SAVE THE RESULT?

YES!! AFTER COMPUTATION, AMPUTATION!

YOU'RE MAD!

EXCUSE ME... I HAVE TO GO PUT MY HANDS TO BETTER USE...

WASH THE WOLF...

SHARPEN ROCKS...

LIKE OTHER ANIMALS, A HUMAN AT FIRST COULD ONLY RETAIN INFORMATION IN THE BRAIN, WHICH HAD A LIMITED CAPACITY. (STILL DOES!!) SO THE HUMAN INVENTED DEVICES TO STORE INFORMATION EXTERNALLY.

THE EARLIEST KNOWN EXAMPLES OF EXTERNAL STORAGE ARE ABOUT 20,000 YEARS OLD, LIKE THIS **TALLY BONE**, APPARENTLY USED TO COUNT THE DAYS OF THE MONTH.

NOW I CAN KEEP TRACK OF MY INTERNAL STORAGE!

AROUND THE SAME TIME, CAVE DWELLERS WERE BEGINNING TO STORE ANOTHER KIND OF INFORMATION AS WELL: THEY PAINTED REALISTIC ANIMALS ON THE WALLS OF THEIR CAVES — NO ONE KNOWS WHY!

SEVERAL THOUSAND YEARS LATER, THE **SUMERIANS** DEVISED A SYSTEM TO REPRESENTING THEIR *ENTIRE LANGUAGE* IN PICTURES:

AND SO WRITING WAS BORN!

UNTIL SOMEONE CAN IMPROVE ON LANGUAGE ITSELF, WRITING WILL BE THE ULTIMATE HUMAN SYSTEM OF INFORMATION STORAGE. IT'S NEARLY UNIVERSAL! PEOPLE ALL AROUND THE WORLD INVENTED SYMBOL SYSTEMS TO ENCODE SPOKEN LANGUAGE. OF COURSE, TECHNIQUES VARIED FROM PLACE TO PLACE...

THE SUMERIANS WROTE ON CLAY TABLETS, WHILE THE EGYPTIANS USED SOFT PAPYRUS.

HM! A FLOPPY TABLET!

CHINESE WRITING BEGAN WITH MESSAGES TO THE GODS INKED ON TORTOISE SHELLS.

THEY DIDN'T ASK THE GOD OF TORTOISES!

THE INCAS USED A SYSTEM OF KNOTTED CORDS.

GREAT! NOW THAT WE'VE **STORED** ALL THAT INFORMATION, HOW DO WE **FIND** IT AGAIN?

WE'LL RETURN TO THAT POINT LATER!

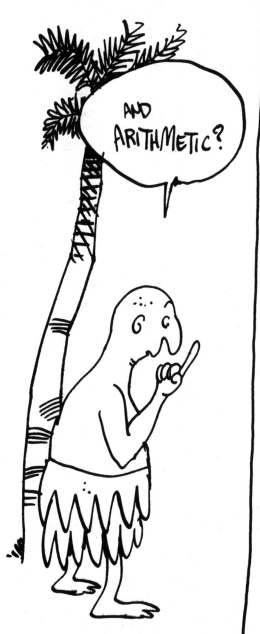

AND ARITHMETIC?

ALL THE EARLY CIVILIZATIONS HAD WAYS OF REPRESENTING NUMBERS THAT WERE FAR ADVANCED OVER THE STONE AGE TALLY BONE, ON WHICH THE NUMBER IS SIMPLY MADE BY PILING UP 1's. NOT TOO USEFUL...

I CALL THIS NUMBER "SMERG."

SOMETIME BETWEEN TALLY BONE AND CIVILIZATION, PEOPLE BECAME ACCUSTOMED TO COUNTING BY *FIVES* AND *TENS* — FOR AN OBVIOUS REASON: IT WAS HANDY.

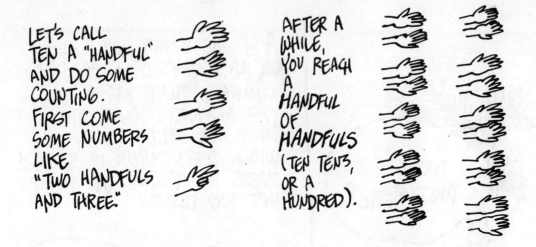

LET'S CALL TEN A "HANDFUL" AND DO SOME COUNTING. FIRST COME SOME NUMBERS LIKE "TWO HANDFULS AND THREE."

AFTER A WHILE, YOU REACH A HANDFUL OF HANDFULS (TEN TENS, OR A HUNDRED).

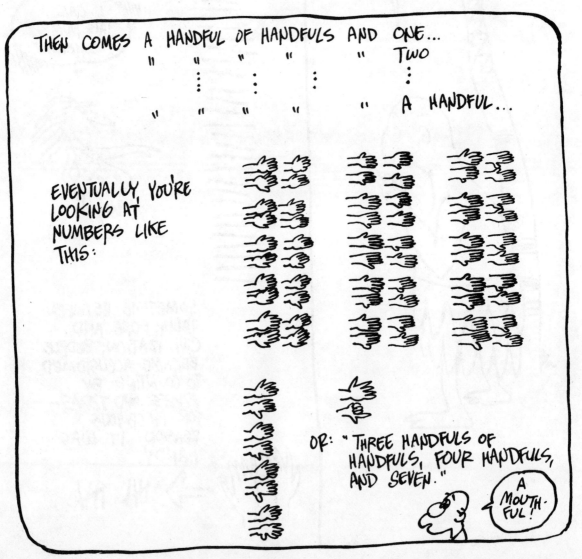

THEN COMES A HANDFUL OF HANDFULS AND ONE...
" " " " " TWO
⋮ ⋮ ⋮ ⋮ ⋮
" " " " " A HANDFUL...

EVENTUALLY, YOU'RE LOOKING AT NUMBERS LIKE THIS:

OR: "THREE HANDFULS OF HANDFULS, FOUR HANDFULS, AND SEVEN."

A MOUTH-FUL!

AND THEN — A HANDFUL OF HANDFULS OF HANDFULS:

THAT'S $10 \times 10 \times 10 = 1000$.

NEXT COMES
   TEN THOUSAND...
   A HUNDRED THOUSAND...
   A THOUSAND THOUSAND...
   TEN THOUSAND THOUSAND...
EACH OF WHICH IS
A *HANDFUL* OF
THE ONE BEFORE!

THIS IS GETTING OUT OF HAND!

T HE ANCIENTS FOUND TWO BASIC WAYS TO TRANSLATE THIS INTO WRITING:

ONE, THE EGYPTIAN SYSTEM, USED A DIFFERENT SYMBOL FOR EACH NEW HANDFUL.

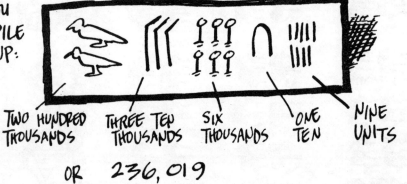

| = ONE   ∩ = TEN   ⟨ = HUNDRED

ϙ = THOUSAND   ⌐ = TEN THOUSAND   🦅 = HUNDRED THOUSAND

THEN YOU JUST PILE THEM UP:

TWO HUNDRED THOUSANDS   THREE TEN THOUSANDS   SIX THOUSANDS   ONE TEN   NINE UNITS

OR   236,019

ASIDE FROM HAVING A CERTAIN GRAPHIC CHARM, THESE NUMERALS ARE VERY EASY TO READ, ONCE YOU'RE USED TO THEM (JUST AS "3 BILLION" READS QUICKER THAN "3000 000 000").

IMPERIAL DEBT TOPS

WHAT'S

TIMES

?

BUT FOR COMPUTATION THEY STINK...

ON THE OTHER HAND, THE CHINESE USED THE *POSITION* OF NUMERALS TO INDICATE THEIR VALUE. FIRST THEY COUNTED FROM ONE TO NINE:

1 2 3 4 5 6 7 8 9

FROM WHICH (FOR EXAMPLE):

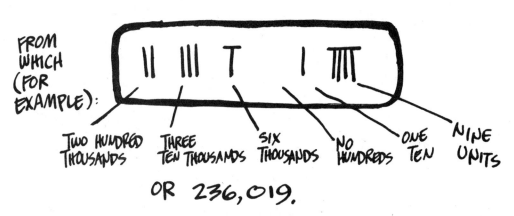

TWO HUNDRED THOUSANDS — THREE TEN THOUSANDS — SIX THOUSANDS — NO HUNDREDS — ONE TEN — NINE UNITS

OR 236,019.

EXCEPT FOR THE UNFAMILIAR NUMERALS, THIS SYSTEM IS NEARLY THE SAME AS OUR OWN.

THE ONLY DIFFERENCE IS THAT IT LACKED A SYMBOL FOR ZERO. THE CHINESE JUST LEFT A BLANK INSTEAD.

HOW MANY SYMBOLS FOR ZERO DO YOU HAVE?

IN PRACTICE, THIS WAS MUCH LESS OF A PROBLEM THAN IT MIGHT HAVE BEEN, BECAUSE THE CHINESE DID NOT CALCULATE ON PAPER !!!

THE CHINESE SYSTEM WAS BASED ON CALCULATION WITH *STICKS.* ONE PILE OF STICKS KEPT TRACK OF THE ONES, ANOTHER THE TENS, ETC. AMONG OTHER THINGS, THIS KEPT THE NUMBER OF STICKS WITHIN REASON.

COUNT BY TENS, SAVE A TREE!

THE WRITTEN NUMERALS WERE JUST DRAWINGS OF THESE "STICK FIGURES."

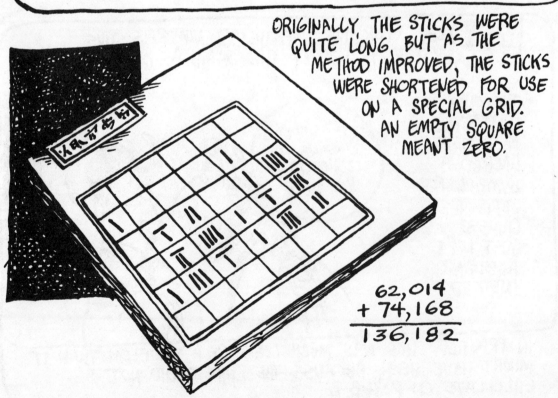

ORIGINALLY, THE STICKS WERE QUITE LONG, BUT AS THE METHOD IMPROVED, THE STICKS WERE SHORTENED FOR USE ON A SPECIAL GRID. AN EMPTY SQUARE MEANT ZERO.

$$62,014$$
$$+ 74,168$$
$$136,182$$

BESIDES ADDITION, SUBTRACTION, MULTIPLICATION AND DIVISION, THIS **SWAN-PAN**, OR "ARITHMETIC TABLE," WAS ALSO APPLIED TO ALGEBRA AND THE SOLUTION OF EQUATIONS. ENTRIES IN THE SQUARES BECAME THE COEFFICIENTS OF ALGEBRAIC EXPRESSIONS.

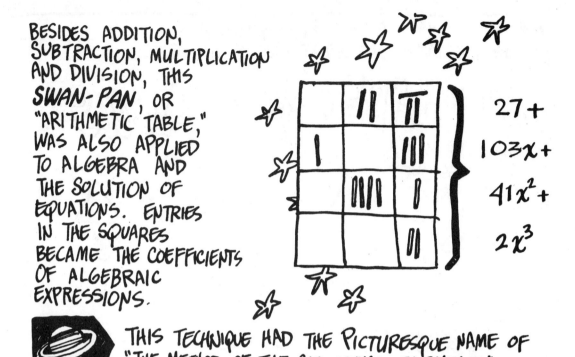

$$27 +$$
$$103x +$$
$$41x^2 +$$
$$2x^3$$

THIS TECHNIQUE HAD THE PICTURESQUE NAME OF "THE METHOD OF THE CELESTIAL ELEMENT."

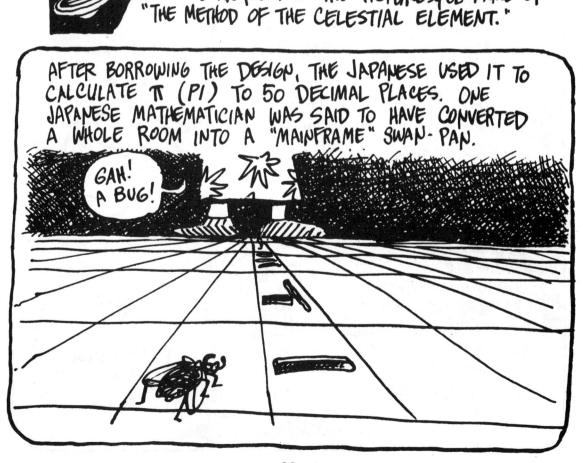

AFTER BORROWING THE DESIGN, THE JAPANESE USED IT TO CALCULATE π (PI) TO 50 DECIMAL PLACES. ONE JAPANESE MATHEMATICIAN WAS SAID TO HAVE CONVERTED A WHOLE ROOM INTO A "MAINFRAME" SWAN-PAN.

GAH! A BUG!

MEANWHILE, BACK AT THE MEDITERRANEAN, THEY HAD MADE TWO GREAT INVENTIONS: THE

ALPHABET & ABACUS.

THE ALPHABET RANKS AS ONE OF THE GREAT IDEAS IN THE HISTORY OF INFORMATION.

$\forall$ $\bowtie$ $\wedge$ $\triangle$

α β γ δ

A   B   C   D

Before

THE ALPHABET, A SEPARATE SYMBOL WAS NEEDED FOR EVERY WORD (OR EVERY SYLLABLE, IN SOME CASES). TO LEARN WRITING, ONE HAD TO MEMORIZE THOUSANDS OF SYMBOLS.

WE CHINESE ARE STILL SADDLED WITH PICTOGRAMS!

After

DECOMPOSING LANGUAGE INTO MORE BASIC SOUNDS, THE NUMBER OF SYMBOLS WAS REDUCED TO FEWER THAN 30. NOW, ANY IDIOT COULD LEARN TO READ!

WHEREAS PREVIOUSLY, ONLY IDIOTS WITH LEISURE COULD LEARN...

THERE'S A LESS OBVIOUS ADVANTAGE OF THE ALPHABET, BUT NO LESS IMPORTANT:

alphabetical order.

DOES 🐦 COME BEFORE OR AFTER 🐁 ?

BACK ON PAGE 22 WE MENTIONED THE PROBLEM OF HOW TO **FIND** INFORMATION ONCE IT'S BEEN STORED.

WITH THOUSANDS OF PICTOGRAMS, ANY FILING SYSTEM HAS TO BE COMPLICATED. BUT GIVEN THE ORDER OF AN ALPHABET, YOU CAN PUT WORDS IN ORDER, TOO. IMAGINE USING A PHONE BOOK, DICTIONARY, OR LIBRARY WITHOUT ALPHABETICAL ORDER!

A VICTIM OF HIS FILING SYSTEM!

COMPUTERS SPEND A GOOD PART OF THEIR TIME JUST PUTTING THINGS IN ORDER!

THE ABACUS, ORIGINALLY A PRODUCT OF THE MIDDLE EAST, IS A FULL-BLOWN HAND-HELD DECIMAL CALCULATOR.

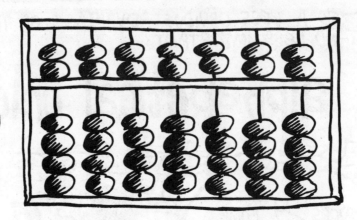

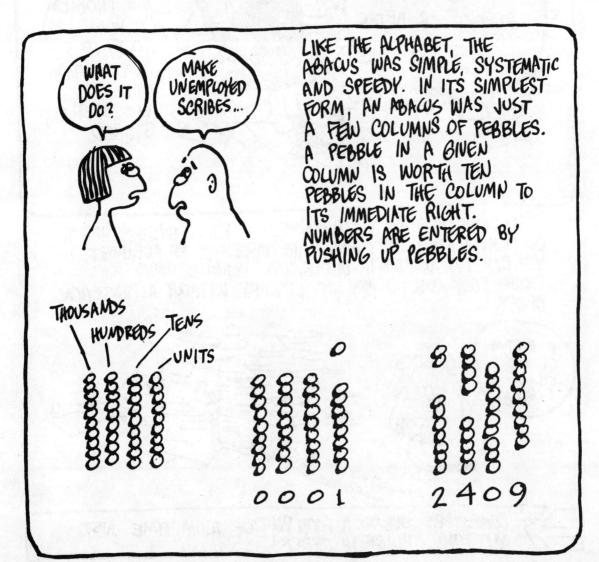

WHAT DOES IT DO?

MAKE UNEMPLOYED SCRIBES...

LIKE THE ALPHABET, THE ABACUS WAS SIMPLE, SYSTEMATIC AND SPEEDY. IN ITS SIMPLEST FORM, AN ABACUS WAS JUST A FEW COLUMNS OF PEBBLES. A PEBBLE IN A GIVEN COLUMN IS WORTH TEN PEBBLES IN THE COLUMN TO ITS IMMEDIATE RIGHT. NUMBERS ARE ENTERED BY PUSHING UP PEBBLES.

THOUSANDS
HUNDREDS TENS
UNITS

0001

2409

THE ABACUS HAS SEEN MANY INCARNATIONS AND BEEN USED IN MOST PARTS OF THE OLD WORLD.

WE KNOW FROM PICTURES THAT THE ANCIENT GREEKS HAD THE ABACUS, BUT THEIR MATHEMATICIANS NEVER DISCUSSED IT. (GREEK INTELLECTUALS LOOKED DOWN ON THE WORK OF THE HANDS...)

THE TOOL OF SHOPKEEPERS!

 THIS MAY HAVE BEEN WHY GREEK MATHEMATICIANS CONCENTRATED ON GEOMETRY...

The Romans

ALSO USED THE ABACUS. THEIRS CONSISTED OF MARBLES SLIDING ON A GROOVED BRONZE PLATE:

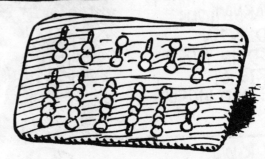

IT CONTRIBUTED A COUPLE OF MATHEMATICAL WORDS TO ENGLISH:

IN LATIN,

CALX

MEANT LIMESTONE OR MARBLE...

$$\frac{1}{2\pi} \int_{-\pi}^{\pi} f(x)\cos x\, dx$$

FROM WHICH COMES "CHALK!"

SO

CALCULUS

WAS AN ABACUS PEBBLE... AND DOING ARITHMETIC WAS

CALCULATION.

THE ROMANS DID NOT CALCULATE WITH ROMAN NUMERALS!!

WHAT'S MXVIII TIMES CLXVI ?

BEATS ME! I LOST MY MARBLES...

...AND FELL...
ROME WAS SACKED...
CHRISTIANITY ROSE
FROM ITS
ASHES... CLASSICAL
LEARNING VANISHED
IN THE WEST...
AND ONLY A FEW
MATH PROBLEMS
REMAINED
LEGITIMATE, LIKE
COMPUTING THE
DATE OF EASTER...
OR HOW MANY
ANGELS FIT ON
THE HEAD OF
A PIN...

ANCIENT TIMES WERE REALLY THE

AGE OF CALCULATORS.

ET TU? ET THREE!

⇒ ALTHOUGH THE ANCIENTS HAD WAYS OF **WRITING** NUMBERS, THEY RARELY CALCULATED IN WRITING.

THIS IS NOT SO EASY TO APPRECIATE FOR THOSE OF US WHO WERE RAISED ON PENCIL AND PAPER.

SO THE NEXT TIME YOU HEAR SOMEONE COMPLAIN THAT **ELECTRONIC** CALCULATORS ARE RUINING ARITHMETIC...

HOW CAN WE REMEMBER OUR MULTIPLICATION TABLES?

...SIMPLY REPLY THAT PEOPLE SURVIVED WITH CALCULATORS FOR MORE THAN 4000 YEARS!!

Much ado about NOTHING

As far as calculation goes, the age of paper began in India, about 650 A.D.

THE INDIANS HAD FOUND A WAY TO MAKE CHEAP PAPER FROM PALM LEAVES, AND THEIR MATHEMATICIANS INVENTED A WAY OF USING IT...

I'VE DISCOVERED NOTHING!

TO DO SO, THEY DEVISED A SYMBOL FOR ZERO!

YOU DISCOVERED WHAT?

WHAT?

NOTHING!

NOTHING, REALLY...

WHAT?

MECHANICAL EQUIVALENTS OF ZERO WERE ALREADY IN USE, SUCH AS ABACUS BEADS SITTING IN THE DOWN POSITION. YOU REALLY CAN'T COMPUTE WITHOUT SOME SORT OF ZERO!

0!

WHY HADN'T ANYONE THOUGHT OF PUTTING IT IN WRITING BEFORE? MAYBE BECAUSE WRITING WAS FOR REPRESENTING SPOKEN LANGUAGE, AND NOBODY SAYS—

ONE HUNDRED, NO TENS AND SIX!

IS THAT PEDANTIC OR VEDANTIC?

BUT FOR SOME REASON, THE HINDUS INVENTED A WRITTEN ZERO!

WE MAY NEVER KNOW EXACTLY WHAT INSPIRED THEM.

I JUST LOOKED IN MY BEGGING BOWL AND THERE IT WAS...

WHATEVER IT WAS, IT ALLOWED THEM TO DO DECIMAL ARITHMETIC ON PAPER.

THE FIRST AND ONLY *DISPOSABLE* CALCULATOR!

AND SO BEGAN THE *AGE OF PENCIL AND PAPER*, A MERE 1300 YEARS AGO — PRETTY BRIEF COMPARED WITH THE AGE OF CALCULATORS!!

AH WELL... EASY COME, EASY GO...

THE INDIAN MATH WAS PICKED UP BY THE **ARABS**, WHO SPREAD IT ALL THE WAY WEST TO SPAIN.

AROUND THE YEAR 830, A PERSIAN SCHOLAR WROTE THE STANDARD TEXTBOOK ON THE SUBJECT. HIS NAME WAS MOHAMMED IBN MUSA ABU DJEFAR, BUT HE WAS KNOWN AS **AL-KHWARISMI.** AND THE SUBJECT OF HIS BOOK?

OR **ALGEBRA**, FOR SHORT.

BY THE 1100'S, MUSLIM CIVILIZATION HAD GROWN SO MAGNIFICENT THAT THE EUROPEANS WERE BEGINNING TO WONDER...

WHY SHOULD GOOD CHRISTIANS REMAIN IN THE DARK AGES?

A FEW INTREPID INFIDELS WENT TO LIVE AMONG THE ARABS, LEARNED THEIR LANGUAGE, SNUCK INTO THEIR UNIVERSITIES, AND TRANSLATED THEIR CLASSICS INTO LATIN.

IN AL-KHWARISMI'S BOOK THEY FOUND THE INDIAN NUMERALS.

AL-KHWARISMI
AL-KARISMI
ALGARISMI
ALGORISMI

PRONOUNCED OFTEN ENOUGH, THE MATHEMATICIAN'S NAME WAS TURNED INTO

ALGORISM—

WHICH IS WHAT THE EUROPEANS CALLED THE NEW SYSTEM OF CALCULATION.

YETH, VERY NITHE...

FROM THE SAME ROOT COMES

ALGORITHM,

A COMPUTER WORD WE'LL EXPLORE IN A BIT...

THIS "ALGORISM" CAUGHT ON ONLY SLOWLY AT FIRST. THE MERCHANTS DISLIKED IT BECAUSE IT WAS TOO EASY TO FALSIFY, THEY SAID...

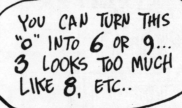

YOU CAN TURN THIS "O" INTO 6 OR 9... 3 LOOKS TOO MUCH LIKE 8, ETC..

THAT'S WHY I LIKE IT!

...AND EVERYONE AGREED IT WAS A PAIN TO MEMORIZE MULTIPLICATION TABLES..

MOAN

BUT IT DID CATCH ON — NOT NECESSARILY BECAUSE IT WAS FASTER THAN THE ABACUS — IT WASN'T — BUT BECAUSE, AS THE ARABS KNEW, IT ENCOURAGES *ABSTRACT SYMBOL-MANIPULATION:* FIRST ALGEBRA, AND LATER THE CALCULUS AND ALL OTHER HIGHER MATHEMATICS.

$$ax + b = 0$$
$$ax = -b$$
$$x = \frac{-b}{a}$$

AND BY THE BYE...

YOU CAN'T COMPUTE ON PAPER WITHOUT HAVING PAPER, SO THE EUROPEANS ALSO LEARNED *PAPERMAKING* FROM THE ARABS, WHO HAD LEARNED IT FROM THE CHINESE, WHO HAD INVENTED IT.

IN EXCHANGE, THE CHINESE TOOK THE **ABACUS** AND RAPIDLY MADE IT THEIR NO. 1 CALCULATOR. FROM CHINA THE ABACUS SPREAD TO JAPAN, WHERE — NEED I SAY IT? — ITS DESIGN WAS IMPROVED!

I THINK WE CAN MAKE IT WITH ONE LESS BEAD...

BUT BACK TO ALGORISM... ⇒

WHILE EUROPEAN SCHOLARS WERE TRANSLATING THE CLASSICS IN ARAB LIBRARIES, THE **CRUSADERS** WERE DOING THEIR BEST TO DESTROY ISLAMIC CIVILIZATION.

IT'S SO MUCH EASIER THAN READING BOOKS!

THIS DOUBLE-PRONGED ACTION OF TRANSLATION AND DESTRUCTION LED TO THE GROWTH OF EUROPEAN LEARNING AND POWER KNOWN AS: The RENAISSANCE.

MILITARY ADVANCES OFTEN GO HAND IN HAND WITH MATHEMATICAL ONES.

EEK!

HA! $y = x^2 + 2x + 3$! GOTCHA!

IN THE 1500's, NICCOLO **TARTAGLIA** (1499-1559) COMPUTED THE PATHS OF CANNONBALLS (AN IMPORTANT PROBLEM IN THE LATER HISTORY OF COMPUTERS, AS WE'LL SEE).

JUST OVER A CENTURY LATER, ISAAC **NEWTON** UNIFIED THE MOTIONS OF CANNONBALLS AND PLANETS WITH THE THEORY OF **GRAVITATION**, ONE OF THE AGE OF PENCIL AND PAPER'S CROWNING GLORIES.

HOWEVER, THE THEORY INTRODUCED SOME REAL COMPUTATIONAL HORRORS...

THE WORST WAS THE **THREE BODY PROBLEM,** WHICH ASKS FOR A MATHEMATICAL DESCRIPTION OF THE MOTIONS OF THREE BODIES — SUN, EARTH, AND MOON, FOR EXAMPLE — ACTING UNDER THE INFLUENCE OF GRAVITY. THIS TURNS OUT TO BE INCREDIBLY DIFFICULT AND TEDIOUS!

WE'RE REACHING THE LIMITS OF PAPER!

SO A NUMBER OF SCIENTISTS BEGAN THINKING AGAIN ABOUT CALCULATION BY **MACHINE...**

John NAPIER, (1550-1617),

A HALF-MAD SCOT MOST FAMOUS FOR LOGARITHMS, DEVISED "NAPIER'S BONES."

THESE WERE SIMPLY MULTIPLICATION TABLES ON A STICK.

THE FIRST REAL MACHINE WAS BUILT BY Wilhelm SCHICKARD (1592 - 1635),

IT COULD ADD, SUBTRACT, MULTIPLY, AND DIVIDE... BUT WAS LOST IN THE 30-YEARS WAR. SCHICKARD HIMSELF DIED OF PLAGUE AND COULDN'T DEFEND HIS PRIORITY, SO...

Blaise PASCAL (1623-1662)

USUALLY GETS CREDIT FOR BUILDING THE FIRST CALCULATOR. HIS "PASCALINE" COULD ONLY ADD AND SUBTRACT.

Gottfried Wilhelm LEIBNIZ (1646-1716)

IMPROVED PASCAL'S DESIGN QUITE A BIT... AND DREAMED OF A DAY WHEN ALL REASONING COULD BE DONE BY TURNING A CRANK!

DURING THE 1700's, MORE SUCH MACHINES WERE BUILT, BUT ALL FELL FAR SHORT OF BEING ANYTHING LIKE A GENERAL-PURPOSE COMPUTER.

FOR EXAMPLE: IN EVERY CASE, THE USER ENTERED NUMBERS BY SETTING A ROW OF WHEELS OR KNOBS...

...AND THEN TURNED THE APPROPRIATE CRANK TO ADD OR MULTIPLY.

ANOTHER WAY OF SAYING THE SAME THING:

THE **INPUT** CONSISTED ONLY OF THE NUMBERS TO BE COMBINED.

AS WILL BE PLAIN SOON ENOUGH, AN ALL-PURPOSE COMPUTER MUST ALSO BE ABLE TO DO MORE: IT MUST READ **INSTRUCTIONS** ABOUT WHAT TO DO WITH THOSE NUMBERS!!

WELL, I WAS ONLY TRYING TO MAKE AN ADDING MACHINE...

48

THE GERM OF THIS IDEA CAME NOT FROM THE LAB OR A SCIENTIST'S STUDY, BUT THE SOOTY FACTORIES OF THE

INDUSTRIAL REVOLUTION

YOU MAY NEVER HAVE THOUGHT OF A *WEAVER'S LOOM* AS AN INFORMATION PROCESSOR, AND YET: IT TRANSLATES AN ABSTRACT DESIGN INTO A PATTERN OF COLORS, CREATED BY LOOPING OVER EACH COLORED THREAD AT THE APPROPRIATE PLACE.

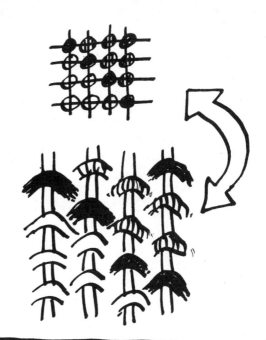

IN THE MID-1700's, A SYSTEM WAS INVENTED FOR REPRESENTING THESE PATTERNS ON PUNCHED CARDS.

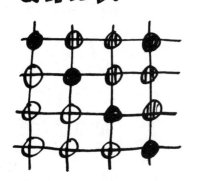

WITH AN OLD FASHIONED
HANDLOOM, THE WEAVER
READ THE CARDS,
BUT IN 1801, JOSEPH MARIE

JACQUARD

INVENTED A POWER
LOOM WITH AN
AUTOMATIC CARD READER.

IN WENT THE CARDS, OUT CAME THE CLOTH...

AND OUT GO
THE JOBS!

THE JACQUARD LOOM WORKED SO WELL THAT THOUSANDS
OF UNEMPLOYED WEAVERS RIOTED AND NEARLY KILLED
THE INVENTOR.

ACROSS THE ENGLISH CHANNEL, JACQUARD'S IDEA SET OFF A CHAIN REACTION IN THE BRAIN OF

CHARLES BABBAGE

(1792-1871),

WHO HAS BECOME KNOWN AS THE "FATHER OF THE COMPUTER."

BY JOVE!!

I SEE NO FAMILY RESEMBLANCE!

FOR SEVERAL YEARS BABBAGE, A CAMBRIDGE MATH PROFESSOR, HAD BEEN WORKING ON A LARGE MECHANICAL CALCULATOR HE CALLED "THE DIFFERENCE ENGINE."

MY ORIGINAL BRAINSTORM...

IT WOULD HAVE COMPUTED MATHEMATICAL TABLES, IF THE INVENTOR HAD EVER BEEN ABLE TO FINISH IT.

IN 1822, BABBAGE APPLIED TO THE ROYAL SOCIETY FOR FUNDS TO BUILD THE DIFFERENCE ENGINE, AND THEY GAVE HIM A SIZABLE GRANT.

HE HIRED A MASTER MACHINIST AND WENT TO WORK... BUT BABBAGE COULDN'T RESIST THINKING UP NEW IMPROVEMENTS IN THE MIDST OF PRODUCTION!

MEANWHILE, HIS HYPERACTIVE MIND KEPT TURNING TO NEW PROJECTS: LIFE INSURANCE TABLES, LIGHTHOUSE SIGNALS, GLASS CUTTING, AND EVEN VOLCANOES. (HE HIKED INTO A LIVE ONE!!)

THAT'S HOW MATTERS STOOD WHEN JACQUARD'S PUNCHED CARDS SET OFF BABBAGE'S NEW BRAINSTORM, A MACHINE HE CALLED:

The ANALYTICAL ENGINE!

BECAUSE IT SO CLOSELY RESEMBLED A COMPUTER, LET'S TAKE A CLOSER LOOK AT THE ANALYTICAL ENGINE, AS BABBAGE IMAGINED IT. ITS COMPONENTS INCLUDED—

THE MILL:

AT THE ENGINE'S HEART WOULD BE A GREAT NUMBER-CRUNCHER, AN ADDING MACHINE ACCURATE TO 50 DECIMAL PLACES. BABBAGE CALLED THIS THE MILL.

HOW DID IT KNOW WHAT TO DO?

THE INSTRUCTIONS TO THE MILL WOULD BE READ IN ON PUNCHCARDS.

THAT IS, THE PUNCHCARDS CONVEYED NOT ONLY THE NUMBERS TO BE CRUNCHED BUT ALSO THE PATTERN OF CRUNCHING!!

SO THE MACHINE WOULD NEED A SPECIAL CARD-READING **INPUT** DEVICE.

TO RETAIN NUMBERS FOR FUTURE REFERENCE, BABBAGE ENVISIONED A MEMORY UNIT, OR **STORE**.

THIS WAS TO BE A BANK OF 1000 "REGISTERS," EACH A DEVICE CAPABLE OF STORING ONE 50-DIGIT NUMBER. THESE NUMBERS COULD EITHER BE INPUT FROM THE CARDS OR THE RESULT OF COMPUTATIONS IN THE MILL.

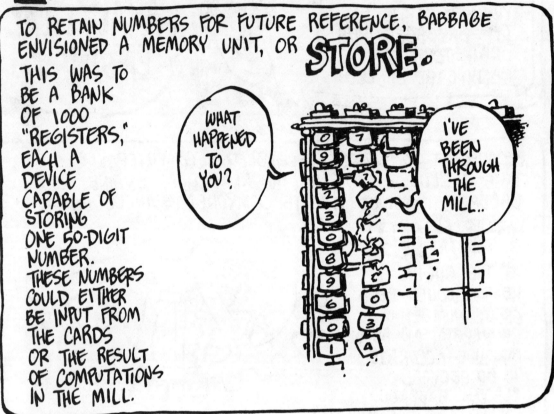

WHAT HAPPENED TO YOU?

I'VE BEEN THROUGH THE MILL...

FINALLY, THE **OUTPUT**:

BABBAGE DESIGNED THE WORLD'S FIRST AUTOMATED TYPE SETTER TO PRINT THE RESULTS OF COMPUTATIONS.

HAVE I FORGOTTEN ANYTHING?

A PUNCHCARD COULD DO ONE OF THE FOLLOWING THINGS:

INPUT A NUMBER TO THE STORE

INPUT A NUMBER TO THE MILL

MOVE A NUMBER FROM THE MILL TO THE STORE

MOVE A NUMBER FROM THE STORE TO THE MILL

INSTRUCT THE MILL TO PERFORM AN OPERATION

OUTPUT A NUMBER FROM EITHER STORE OR MILL

WHICH MAY BE SUMMARIZED IN THIS DIAGRAM:

INPUT

MILL

STORE

OUTPUT

IN PARTICULAR, A RESULT FROM THE MILL COULD BE STORED FOR FUTURE REFERENCE, THEN RETURNED TO THE MILL WHEN NEEDED. AS BABBAGE PUT IT, THE ANALYTICAL ENGINE COULD "EAT ITS OWN TAIL." VERY FLEXIBLE!

YOU HAVE TO BE FLEXIBLE TO EAT YOUR OWN TAIL...

SO FAR, THESE IDEAS WERE STILL ON THE DRAWING BOARD. NOW BABBAGE BEGAN LOOKING FOR SYMPATHETIC SOULS WHO COULD HELP PUT HIS PLANS INTO OPERATION.

THE MOST SYMPATHETIC WAS

ADA AUGUSTA,

LADY LOVELACE, DAUGHTER OF THE POET LORD BYRON AND AN ENTHUSIASTIC AMATEUR MATHEMATICIAN. IF CHARLES BABBAGE IS THE COMPUTER'S FATHER, ADA LOVELACE IS ITS MOTHER!!

ADA BECAME THE FIRST **PROGRAMMER**: SHE WROTE OUT ACTUAL SEQUENCES OF INSTRUCTIONS FOR THE ANALYTICAL ENGINE...

TOO BAD IT DOESN'T EXIST YET...

SHE INVENTED THE SUBROUTINE: A SEQUENCE OF INSTRUCTIONS WHICH CAN BE USED AGAIN AND AGAIN IN MANY CONTEXTS.

WE CAN HAVE A WHOLE LIBRARY OF THEM!

SHE RECOGNIZED THE VALUE OF LOOPING: THERE SHOULD BE AN INSTRUCTION THAT BACKS UP THE CARD READER TO A SPECIFIED CARD, SO THAT THE SEQUENCE IT INITIATES CAN BE EXECUTED REPEATEDLY.

"GO TO CARD #7"

AND SHE DREAMED UP THE CONDITIONAL JUMP: THE CARD READER COULD "JUMP" TO ANOTHER CARD IF SOME CONDITION IS SATISFIED.

IF A=B

IT CAN MAKE DECISIONS!

NOT BAD FOR A MACHINE THAT NEVER EXISTED... THE GOVERNMENT REFUSED TO SUPPORT IT, IN VIEW OF BABBAGE'S TRACK RECORD WITH THE DIFFERENCE ENGINE THEY CALLED IT:

DESPERATE FOR FUNDS, BABBAGE COOKED UP A "SCIENTIFIC" RACETRACK BETTING SCHEME — AND SQUANDERED ADA'S FORTUNE.

THE STORY ENDED UNHAPPILY: ADA DIED YOUNG... AND BABBAGE NEVER FINISHED THE ANALYICAL ENGINE, WHICH BECAME THE FIRST EXAMPLE OF—

THE ILL-STARRED INVENTORS WERE AHEAD OF THEIR TIME. NOTHING EQUIVALENT TO THE ANALYTICAL ENGINE EXISTED UNTIL THE 1940's.

ALMOST AS LATE AS OUR HORSE...

IN THE MEANTIME, MATTERS PROGRESSED IN TWO DIRECTIONS:

ON THE ONE HAND WERE MECHANICAL CALCULATORS: SEVERAL ENGINEERS BUILT BABBAGE-INSPIRED DIFFERENCE ENGINES. FOR SOME REASON, THESE NEVER CAUGHT ON...

YOU DON'T **WANT** TO COMPUTE x^2+x+41 IN YOUR VERY OWN LIVING ROOM?

WOW! SOUND EFFECTS!

DING

...ALTHOUGH DESKTOP ADDING MACHINES AND CASH REGISTERS DID BECOME FIXTURES IN BUSINESS.

ON THE OTHER HAND WERE THE PUNCHCARD MACHINES, BEGINNING WITH THE CENSUS TABULATORS DESIGNED BY **HERMAN HOLLERITH** (1860-1929).

INSPIRED, AS BABBAGE HAD BEEN, BY THE JACQUARD LOOM, HOLLERITH INVENTED A MACHINE PURELY FOR ACCUMULATING AND CLASSIFYING INFORMATION.

BECAUSE THIS WAS A NEW SORT OF JOB FOR A MACHINE— AND THE KIND FOR WHICH COMPUTERS ARE IDEALLY SUITED— LET'S TOOK A CLOSER LOOK.

BEFORE HOLLERITH, THE CENSUS BUREAU PROCESSED ALL DATA BY HAND...SLOWLY. THE 1880 CENSUS TOOK **7½** YEARS TO ANALYZE!

THIS IS A LITTLE LIKE PREDICTING YESTERDAY'S WEATHER...

THEN AS NOW, THE CENSUS FORM CONSISTED OF A SERIES OF MULTIPLE CHOICE QUESTIONS...

HOW MANY CHILDREN DO YOU HAVE?
a) 0-2   b) 3-7   c) 8-20
   d) MORE THAN 20
WHAT'S YOUR RELIGIOUS PREFERENCE?
a) MILITANT HINDU   b) I.W.W.
c) FUNDAMENTALIST VEGETARIAN   d) OTHER
ETC...

FROM THIS, ONE WANTED TO FIND:

THE TOTAL NUMBER OF CITIZENS...

HOW MANY HAD 0-2 CHILDREN...

HOW MANY WERE MILITANT HINDUS... ETC!

AS WELL AS SUCH THINGS AS:

HOW MANY FUNDAMENTALIST VEGETARIANS HAVE MORE THAN 20 CHILDREN?

HOLLERITH PROPOSED TO PUT EACH PERSON'S RESPONSES ON A SINGLE PUNCHED CARD THE SIZE OF AN 1880 DOLLAR BILL. TO OVER-SIMPLIFY SLIGHTLY, EACH COLUMN REPRESENTED ONE QUESTION. THE HOLE IN A GIVEN COLUMN INDICATED THE ANSWER TO THAT QUESTION.

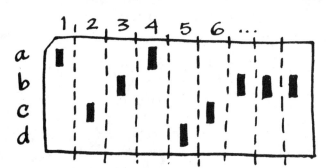

THIS CARD SHOWS RESPONSES OF 1-a, 2-c, 3-b, 4-a, 5-d, ETC...

THE CARDS WERE "READ" BY A DEVICE CONSISTING OF A GRID OF LITTLE PINS MOUNTED ON SPRINGS AND WIRED ELECTRICALLY.

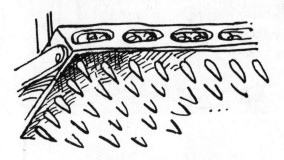

EACH CUP WAS WIRED TO A COUNTER, WHICH ADVANCED EACH TIME AN ELECTRIC PULSE ARRIVED.

WHEN BROUGHT INTO CONTACT WITH THE CARD, ONLY THOSE PINS LYING OVER A HOLE WOULD PASS THROUGH. EACH OF THESE DIPPED INTO A SMALL CUP OF MERCURY, COMPLETING AN ELECTRICAL CIRCUIT.

AND SO THE RUNNING TOTALS OF EVERY POSSIBLE RESPONSE WERE CONTINUOUSLY DISPLAYED!

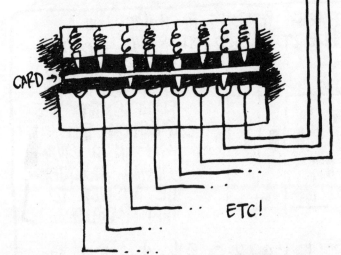

CARD→

ETC!

DOES IT COUNT UNEMPLOYED CENSUS WORKERS?

THE TABULATOR ALSO HELPED ANSWER QUESTIONS SUCH AS: "HOW MANY PEOPLE WHO ANSWERED 2-a ALSO ANSWERED 3-c?"

MEANING: HOW MANY MILITANT HINDUS LIVE IN KANSAS?

HERE'S HOW:

FIRST, ARRANGE A BELL TO RING WHENEVER A CARD WITH 2-a IS ENTERED.

THEN RUN THROUGH ALL CARDS, PULLING OUT ALL THOSE THAT RING THE BELL.

THIS CREATES A STACK OF ALL THE MILITANT HINDU CARDS. RUN THESE THROUGH THE TABULATOR AGAIN.

THE MACHINE THEN SHOWS ALL THE TOTALS FOR MILITANT HINDUS.

HOW MANY DO LIVE IN KANSAS?

ZERO!

THIS SORT OF JOB — ANALYZING AND COMPARING LARGE AMOUNTS OF INFORMATION — IS NOW KNOWN AS:

DATA PROCESSING.

THE HOLLERITH TABULATOR CUT THE DATA PROCESSING TIME FOR THE 1890 CENSUS BY **TWO THIRDS**, TO $2\frac{1}{2}$ YEARS. THIS SOUNDS LONG NOW, BUT AT THE TIME, IT WAS IMPRESSIVE!!

WOW!

HOLLERITH FOUNDED A COMPANY TO MANUFACTURE HIS CARD-OPERATED DATA PROCESSORS, AND HE FOUND A NUMBER OF TAKERS:

A RAILROAD COMPANY USED THE TABULATOR FOR AUDITING FREIGHT STATISTICS...
A TOOL MANUFACTURER TURNED IT TO COMPILING COSTS, ANALYZING PAYROLL, AND MANAGING INVENTORY...
A WHOLESALE HOUSE NEEDED IT TO KEEP TRACK OF MERCHANDISE, SALES, SALESMEN, CUSTOMERS, ETC ETC ETC...

THIS COMPANY IS GOING SOMEWHERE!

"SO" HOLLERITH'S COMPANY DID FAIRLY WELL... LATER, IT GOT INTO COMPUTERS, TOO... AND DID WELL... YOU MAY HAVE HEARD OF IT... TODAY IT'S CALLED **IBM.**

SO BIG, IT DOESN'T FIT IN THE PANEL!

IN THE MIDST OF ALL THIS COMPLEX CIRCUITRY SOME RESEARCHERS FOCUSED ON THE SIMPLEST ELECTRICAL PART OF ALL:

THE **SWITCH**

A SWITCH IS ANY KIND OF DEVICE WHICH CAN OPEN OR CLOSE AN ELECTRIC CIRCUIT.

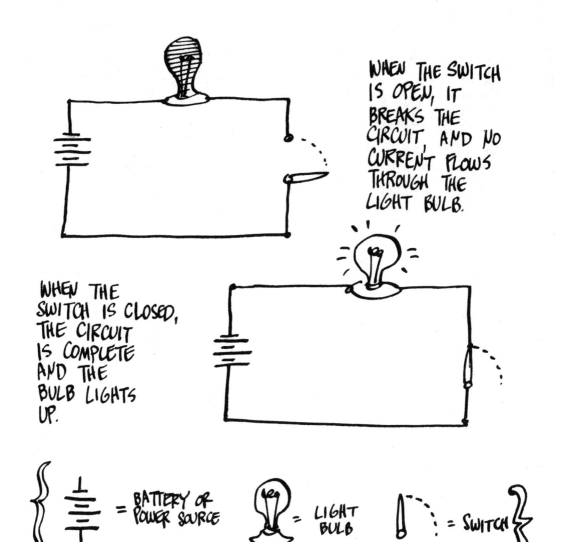

WHEN THE SWITCH IS OPEN, IT BREAKS THE CIRCUIT, AND NO CURRENT FLOWS THROUGH THE LIGHT BULB.

WHEN THE SWITCH IS CLOSED, THE CIRCUIT IS COMPLETE AND THE BULB LIGHTS UP.

$\left\{ \vphantom{}\right.$ ⊥ = BATTERY OR POWER SOURCE 💡 = LIGHT BULB 🔪⋯ = SWITCH $\left. \vphantom{}\right\}$

A FEW FAMILIAR SWITCHES:

TOGGLE SWITCHES

ROTARY SWITCHES

OFF
ON

OFF ON
PUSHBUTTON SWITCHES

A LESS FAMILIAR SWITCH IS THE

TELEPHONE

SWITCH. YOU CAN'T SEE IT, BUT IT COMPLETES THE CONNECTION BETWEEN YOUR PHONE AND THE ONE YOU'VE DIALED.

IN THE OLD DAYS, THIS HAD TO BE DONE BY HAND —

THE OPERATOR'S WORK STATION WAS CALLED A

SWITCHBOARD, AFTER ALL!

THEN THE PHONE CO., IN ITS WISDOM, CAME UP WITH THE AUTOMATIC **RELAY**. ON RECEIVING AN ELECTRIC SIGNAL, THIS SWITCH WOULD CLOSE AND "RELAY" YOUR CALL TO THE RIGHT PLACE.

THE TELEPHONE RELAY COULD SWITCH MUCH FASTER THAN THE HUMAN HAND — ABOUT **5** TIMES PER SECOND! IT MADE THE SWITCHBOARD OPERATOR OBSOLETE...

GUESS I'LL APPLY FOR A JOB AT THE RELAY WORKS...

BUT IT COULDN'T HOLD A CANDLE TO ANOTHER TYPE OF SWITCH INVENTED EVEN EARLIER: THE VACUUM TUBE.

REMEMBER WHEN TUBES USED TO GLOW IN THE BACK OF THE RADIO? YOU DON'T? SIGH....

THE TUBE CAN ALSO BE FLIPPED ON AND OFF LIKE A SWITCH, SO FAST YOU CAN'T EVEN SEE IT FLICKER: IT JUST GLOWS... BUT IT CAN SWITCH AS OFTEN AS

1,000,000
TIMES PER SECOND!!!

WOW

NOW HERE'S THE KEY:

NOT LONG AFTER THESE SWITCHES WERE INVENTED, PEOPLE REALIZED THAT THEY COULD BE COMBINED INTO COMPUTER COMPONENTS!

THAT IS,

PATTERNS OF SWITCHES CAN BE ARRANGED TO **ADD,** TO **STORE,** AND EVEN TO EMBODY **LOGICAL RELATIONSHIPS** (WHATEVER THAT MEANS). DETAILS LATER!

IF I INSERT FINGER **AND** FLIP THIS SWITCH, **THEN** I AM A DEAD ENGINEER!

BY THE 1930'S, A NUMBER OF PEOPLE HAD SEEN HOW VERY RAPID COMPUTERS COULD BE BUILT FROM HARDWARE STRAIGHT OFF THE SHELF!!

TUNA? SOUP? CANNED SPAGHETTI?

DESPITE THE TUBE'S FANTASTIC SWITCHING SPEED, THE FIRST ELECTRONIC COMPUTING MACHINES USED ELECTROMECHANICAL SWITCHES LIKE RELAYS, BECAUSE THEY WERE MORE RELIABLE.

TUBES GET TOO HOT AND BURN OUT!

REMINDS ME OF MY EX-HUSBAND...

Who built

THE FIRST ELECTROMECHANICAL COMPUTER? THE VERY FIRST WAS **KONRAD ZUSE** (1910 -).

HIS Z·1, BUILT IN 1936, CALCULATED WITH RELAYS AND READ INPUT FROM PUNCHED FILM.

ZUSE, A GERMAN, TRIED TO SELL THE Z·1 TO HIS GOVERNMENT FOR WAR WORK.

IT CAN PLAY "BATTLE OF BRITAIN"! "FRENCH INVADERS"! "STALINGRAD"!

THE NAZIS ASSUMED THEY HAD "ALL BUT" WON THE WAR, SO THEY TURNED HIM DOWN... AND POSSIBLY CHANGED HISTORY!!

ACH!

THE COMPUTER WAS REALLY BORN WITH

WORLD WAR II!

(NOTE ROMAN NUMERAL!)

IN THE USA, THE NAVY COLLABORATED WITH HARVARD AND IBM TO CONSTRUCT THE MARK I, AN ELECTROMAGNETIC GIANT LAUNCHED IN 1944.

DESIGNED BY HARVARD PROF HOWARD AIKEN, WHO MODELED IT ON BABBAGE'S ANALYTICAL ENGINE, MARK I OCCUPIED SOME 1200 CUBIC FEET AND CONTAINED THOUSANDS OF RELAYS. WHEN IT CRANKED UP, THEY SAY IT SOUNDED LIKE A MILLION KNITTING NEEDLES!!

EXCUSE ME SIR! I'M GOING MAD SIR!

MARK I COULD MULTIPLY TWO 10-DIGIT NUMBERS (A CONVENIENT MEASURE OF COMPUTER SPEED) IN ABOUT **3 SECONDS.**

AN UNHEARD-OF SPEED!

UNBEKNOWNST TO THE NAVY, THE ARMY WAS ALSO FUNDING A COMPUTER PROJECT — ONLY THEIRS WOULD USE TUBES!

WE'LL SHOW THEM NAVY WIMPS!

THEIR AIM WAS THE SAME AS TARTAGLIA'S IN THE 1500'S: TO COMPUTE **BALLISTICS** MORE ACCURATELY.

TARTAGLIA HAD ERRED IN SAYING THAT CANNON-BALLS FLY IN PARABOLIC PATHS. IN REALITY, AIR RESISTANCE ALTERS THEIR TRAJECTORY APPRECIABLY, AND IN A VERY COMPLEX WAY, BECAUSE AIR RESISTANCE DIMINISHES AT HIGHER ALTITUDES.

IN WORLD WAR I, THE GERMAN CANNON "BIG BERTHA" SHOT 94 MILES — TWICE AS FAR AS EXPECTED FROM OVERSIMPLIFIED CALCULATIONS!

GUNNERS AND BOMBARDIERS THEREFORE NEEDED ACCURATE **BALLISTIC TABLES** TO AIM BY. THESE COULD HARDLY BE CALCULATED ON THE FLY!

A LITTLE TO THE LEFT— NO...

BALLISTIC TABLES USED TO BE CALCULATED BY ROOMFULS OF "GIRLS" WITH ADDING MACHINES — AND EVEN THIS WAS SLOW.

WHAT DID YOU DO BEFORE?

TELEPHONE OPERATOR...

THE CHIEF ENGINEERS IN THE ARMY PROJECT WERE **J. PRESPER ECKERT** AND **JOHN MAUCHLY.**

MAUCHLY

ECKERT

THE RESULT OF THEIR LABORS WAS THE BARN-SIZED **ENIAC:** THE **E**LECTRONIC **N**UMERICAL **I**NTEGRATOR **A**ND **C**ALCULATOR. WITH 18,000 TUBES, ENIAC WAS *FAST:*

500 MULTIPLICATIONS PER SECOND!

(IT ALSO NEEDED ITS OWN AIR-CONDITIONING SYSTEM!)

THE ONLY PROBLEM WITH ENIAC WAS THAT IT WASN'T COMPLETED UNTIL 1946, SEVERAL MONTHS AFTER THE WAR WAS OVER!

≳SIGH≲ IT'S BABBAGE'S LAW!

BEST THING ABOUT WAR IS THERE'S ALWAYS ANOTHER!

SO THE ARMY PUT ENIAC TO WORK ON THE NEXT WAR, DOING CALCULATIONS FOR THE NUCLEAR WEAPONS PROGRAM...

ENIAC MAY HAVE BEEN FAST, BUT IN SOME WAYS IT WAS PRETTY DUMB. ITS MEMORY WAS VERY SMALL, AND EACH NEW CALCULATION REQUIRED A WHOLE CHANGE OF WIRING.

IN OTHER WORDS, IT'S PROGRAMMED BY SCREWDRIVER!

BUT STILL IMPRESSIVE: WITH 18,000 TUBES FLICKERING ON AND OFF 100,000 TIMES PER SECOND, ENIAC HAD TO PERFORM FAR MORE RELIABLY THAN ANY MACHINE EVER CONSTRUCTED.

MISCALCULATION COULD BE FATAL!

NOW ENTERS **JOHN VON NEUMANN** (1903-1957), A PRINCETON MATH PROFESSOR WHO MORE THAN ANYONE GETS CREDIT FOR TURNING ELECTRONIC CALCULATORS INTO "ELECTRONIC BRAINS."

VON NEUMANN PONDERED THE COMPUTER'S *LOGICAL STRUCTURE* IN THE ABSTRACT: HOW IT CONTROLS ITSELF, HOW MUCH MEMORY IT NEEDS AND WHAT FOR, ETC... AND HE ASKED HIMSELF HOW COMPUTERS COULD BE MADE MORE LIKE HUMAN "WIRING," I.E., THE CENTRAL NERVOUS SYSTEM.

OH, THE INPUT BONE CONNECTED TO THE MEMORY BONE...

CONSIDER HOW A HUMAN BEING "RUNS A PROGRAM":
WHEN A SURGEON STARTS TO CUT, IT SHOULDN'T BE NECESSARY TO KEEP REFERRING BACK TO THE TEXTBOOK FOR INSTRUCTIONS.

No... FIRST THE SURGEON GOES TO MEDICAL SCHOOL, READS THE PROCEDURES, AND COMMITS THEM TO MEMORY.

"STEP 2: GROPE AROUND FOR TUMOR."

"STEP 3: CALL YOUR BROKER...."

THIS SPEEDS UP SURGERY CONSIDERABLY!

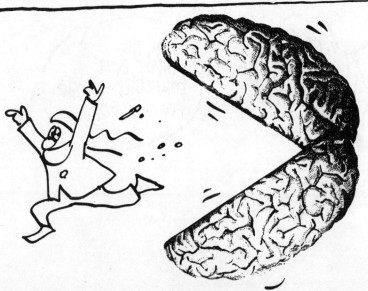

YOUR BRAIN IS FULL OF THESE "STORED PROGRAMS": YOU KNOW HOW TO TIE YOUR SHOELACES, HOW TO FEED YOURSELF, HOW TO MULTIPLY 94 TIMES 16, HOW TO TALK, HOW TO WALK...

VON NEUMANN PROPOSED TO MAKE COMPUTERS DO LIKEWISE:

1. FIND A WAY TO **ENCODE** THE INSTRUCTIONS INTO A FORM WHICH COULD BE STORED IN THE COMPUTER'S MEMORY. VON NEUMANN SUGGESTED USING STRINGS OF ONES AND ZEROS.

2. STORE THE INSTRUCTIONS IN MEMORY, ALONG WITH WHATEVER OTHER INFORMATION (NUMBERS, ETC) IS NEEDED TO DO THE PARTICULAR JOB.

3. WHEN RUNNING THE PROGRAM, FETCH THE INSTRUCTIONS STRAIGHT FROM MEMORY, RATHER THAN READING A NEW PUNCHCARD AT EACH STEP.

THIS IS THE CONCEPT OF THE

STORED PROGRAM.

The advantages?

SPEED:
LIKE THE SURGEON, THE COMPUTER FINDS IT MUCH FASTER TO WHIZ INSTRUCTIONS FROM "BRAIN" TO "FINGERS" THAN TO "RETURN TO THE TEXTBOOK" AFTER EXECUTING EACH STEP.

VERSATILITY:
WITH SEVERAL PROGRAMS STORED AT ONCE, THEY CAN REFER TO ONE ANOTHER RUNNING IN COMBINATION. SURGERY IS ACTUALLY SUCH A COMBINATION.

SELF-MODIFICATION:
IF STORED ELECTRONICALLY, PROGRAMS MAY EASILY BE WRITTEN WHICH CAN MODIFY OR ADJUST THEMSELVES. THIS TURNS OUT TO BE CRITICALLY IMPORTANT!

TO MAKE HIS POINT, VON NEUMANN WROTE SOME CODE FOR A PROGRAM CALLED:

SORT AND MERGE

IT'S A SIMPLE JOB TO DESCRIBE:

GIVEN TWO LISTS OF NAMES (FOR EXAMPLE):

```
ALABAMA, S.
ANTEATER, J.
ANTEATER, B.
AARDVARK, A.
```

```
TARDIGRADE, C.
BEAVER, M.
OWL, H.
ALLIGATOR, A.
```

```
AARDVARK, A.
ALABAMA, S.
ALLIGATOR, A.
ANTEATER, B.
ANTEATER, J.
BEAVER, M.
OWL, H.
TARDIGRADE, C.
```

MAKE ONE LIST IN ALPHABETICAL ORDER.

THIS SEEMINGLY SIMPLE PROCESS BECOMES HORRIBLY TIME-CONSUMING WHEN THE LISTS ARE LONG.

SO:
HERE'S ANOTHER IDEAL COMPUTER JOB THAT CONTAINS ESSENTIALLY NO MATH. YOU CAN SEE HOW THIS ONE MIGHT APPEAL TO SOMEONE COMPILING A TELEPHONE DIRECTORY OR A MAILING LIST!!

O THANK YOU THANK YOU..

ACTUALLY, THERE'S SOME ARGUMENT OVER WHO INVENTED THE STORED PROGRAM. ECKERT AND MAUCHLY CLAIMED CREDIT, TOO... AND THE **ENIAC** PROJECT DISSOLVED IN A WELTER OF LAWSUITS OVER WHO OWNED WHAT IDEA...

STORED PROGRAMS ARE WHAT SEPARATE TRUE COMPUTERS FROM EVERYTHING PRE-*ENIAC*.

IF COMPUTERS HAD REMAINED AS BULKY AS **ENIAC**, THEY WOULDN'T BE WHAT THEY ARE TODAY... BUT THEY DIDN'T, AND THEY ARE...

IN 1947, THE YEAR AFTER **ENIAC** WAS FINISHED, A TEAM AT STANFORD INVENTED THE **TRANSISTOR**, USING ELEMENTS CALLED **SEMICONDUCTORS**.

LIKE TUBES, TRANSISTORS CAN ACT AS SWITCHES, BUT THEY'RE

SMALLER, FASTER, COOLER, AND LONGER-LIVED, AND THEY DRAW FAR LESS ELECTRIC POWER.

THE FIRST TRANSISTORIZED COMPUTERS WERE ROOM-SIZED, NOT BARN-SIZED, AND THEIR COST (A COUPLE OF MILLION DOLLARS) WAS AFFORDABLE BY LARGE BUSINESSES AND UNIVERSITIES.

AND SO "COMPUTER ERROR" ENTERED EVERYDAY LIFE!

PHONE BILL
10056.00

THEN THE TRANSISTOR BEGAN TO SHOW AN INCREDIBLE ABILITY TO SHRINK IN SIZE AND PRICE.

FIRST CAME **INTEGRATED CIRCUITS** — A WHOLE BOARDFUL OF TRANSISTORS MANUFACTURED AS A SINGLE UNIT... THEN **LARGE-SCALE** AND **VERY LARGE-SCALE INTEGRATION** (LSI AND VSLI), WHICH PACKED HUNDREDS OF THOUSANDS OF TRANSISTORS ON A TINY CHIP!

HMPH! BUGS!

 AS COMPONENTS SHRANK, THE INDUSTRY EXPLODED!

IN THE '60'S, THE **MINICOMPUTER** APPEARED. IT WAS THE SIZE OF A DESK!

MAKES IT LESS MYSTERIOUS SOMEHOW!

IN THE '70'S CAME THE **MICRO**, WHICH CAN BE AS SMALL AS YOU LIKE.

WHAT'S NEXT? THE DISPOSABLE?

BY THIS TIME, BIG COMPUTERS, ALSO KNOWN AS **MAINFRAMES**, HAD BECOME IMMENSELY POWERFUL.

100,000 TRANSISTORS PER CHIP... 100,000 CHIPS PER MACHINE...

AND FINALLY THE EXOTIC **SUPERCOMPUTERS**, WHICH CALCULATE AT RATES UP TO 500 *MEGAFLOPS* — A MILLION TIMES FASTER THAN ENIAC!

* MILLION FLOATING POINT OPERATIONS PER SECOND.

THERE'S NO END IN SIGHT.... NOW WE HAVE MICROS WITH THE POWER OF MINIS, "SUPERMINIS" THAT RIVAL MAINFRAMES, MINIS ON A CHIP... AND THERE'S TALK OF REDUCING COMPONENTS TO MOLECULAR SIZE USING RECOMBINANT DNA TECHNOLOGY...

IT MAKES ME FEEL GROSSLY LARGE...

THERE SEEMS TO BE NO SUCH THING AS A COMPUTER WITH TOO MUCH COMPUTING POWER. NO MATTER THE SPEED OR CAPACITY, COMPUTERS ALWAYS FIND JOBS TO DO... AND NO WONDER: THIS IS THE AGE OF EXCESS INFORMATION!

PART II

LOGICAL SPAGHETTI

Computers are like elephants: there are a lot of ways to describe them...

A powerful calculator!

Made of switches!

It follows instructions!

An input-output device!

Exotic hardware!

How does one get to the heart of the matter?

With an elephant cleaver?

IF THERE'S ONE IDEA WE'VE TRIED TO DRUM IN, IT'S THAT THE COMPUTER IS ESSENTIALLY AN **INFORMATION PROCESSOR.** SO FORGET THE ELEPHANT...

TO UNDERSTAND INFORMATION PROCESSING, IT HELPS TO COMPARE IT WITH A MORE FAMILIAR PROCESS: *COOKING.* SO STEP INTO GRANDMOTHER BABBAGE'S KITCHEN, AS SHE PREPARES BASIC SPAGHETTI...

HERE'S THE WORLD FAMOUS RECIPE:

 BRING A KETTLE OF SALTED WATER TO BOIL.

 ADD 8 OZ. OF RAW SPAGHETTI.

 BOIL FOR 10 MINUTES.

 DRAIN THROUGH A SIEVE.

 SERVE..

THIS SPAGHETTI IS BETTER ANALYZED THAN EATEN!

IT'S NOT HARD TO DISTINGUISH A FEW COMPONENTS IN THIS PROCESS:

FIRST, THE INGREDIENTS, OR **INPUT.**

 DRY SPAGHETTI

 WATER

 SALT

NEXT, THE EQUIPMENT WHICH DOES THE COOKING: HANDS, KETTLE, STOVE, SALTSHAKER, SIEVE, PLATE, SPOON.

THESE FORM THE **PROCESSING UNIT.**

LESS OBVIOUSLY, THERE IS A **PART OF THE COOK'S BRAIN** WHICH **CONTROLS** THE PROCESS. IT MONITORS AND DIRECTS THE STEP-BY-STEP UNFOLDING OF THE RECIPE. THIS IS REFERRED TO AS THE **CONTROL UNIT.**

AND OF COURSE THE COMPLETED DISH, OR **OUTPUT.**

WHICH ALSO RESEMBLES THE COOK'S BRAIN...

OF COURSE, SPAGHETTI IS NOTHING SPECIAL! ANY RECIPE COULD BE PROCESSED BY THE SAME BASIC STRUCTURE:

INGREDIENTS OR INPUT $\Rightarrow$ A PROCESSING UNIT UNDER CONTROL $\Rightarrow$ OUTPUT

UGH! WHAT IS THIS ★#◐?

OR, MORE ABSTRACTLY:

CONTROL

INPUT $\Rightarrow$ PROCESSING UNIT $\Rightarrow$ OUTPUT

WHITE ARROWS ($\Rightarrow$) ARE THE FLOW OF FOOD
GRAY ARROW ($\Rightarrow$) IS THE FLOW OF INFORMATION
BLACK ARROW ($\rightarrow$) IS THE FLOW OF CONTROL.

WITH COMPUTERS, THE DIAGRAM IS SLIGHTLY DIFFERENT:

THERE ARE TWO REASONS
FOR THIS: ONE IS THE
FACT THAT INPUT AND
OUTPUT ARE INFORMATION,
NOT FOOD — SO THE
GRAY ARROW IS THE
SAME AS THE WHITE
ONES.

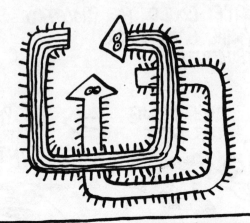

THE OTHER IS THE GREAT IMPORTANCE OF MEMORY,
WHICH FORMS THE FIFTH AND FINAL
COMPONENT. IN COMPUTERS, ALL INFORMATION
PASSES INTO MEMORY FIRST! HERE'S THE DIAGRAM:

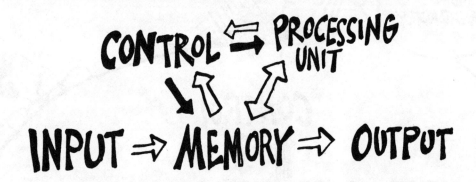

CONTROL ⇨ PROCESSING UNIT

INPUT ⇨ MEMORY ⇨ OUTPUT

⇨ = INFORMATION FLOW   ➡ = CONTROL FLOW

VON NEUMANN'S IDEA:

IN THE CASE OF COMPUTERS, THE **INPUT** CONSISTS OF ALL THE "RAW" DATA TO BE PROCESSED — **AS WELL AS** THE ENTIRE "RECIPE," OR PROGRAM, WHICH SPECIFIES WHAT'S TO BE DONE WITH THEM.

THE **MEMORY** STORES THE INPUT AND RESULTS FROM THE PROCESSING UNIT:

CONTROL READS THE PROGRAM AND TRANSLATES IT INTO A SEQUENCE OF MACHINE OPERATIONS.

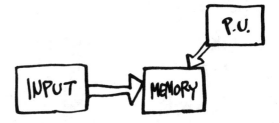

THE **PROCESSING UNIT** PERFORMS THE ACTUAL ADDITION, MULTIPLICATION, COUNTING, COMPARISON, ETC, ON INFORMATION RECEIVED FROM MEMORY.

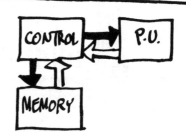

THE **OUTPUT** CONSISTS OF THE PROCESSING UNIT'S RESULTS, STORED IN MEMORY AND TRANSMITTED TO AN OUTPUT DEVICE.

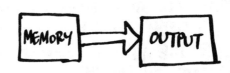

HERE'S THE REAL THING (AN IBM PERSONAL COMPUTER), JUST TO GIVE ONE EXAMPLE OF HOW THESE COMPONENTS MAY ACTUALLY LOOK:

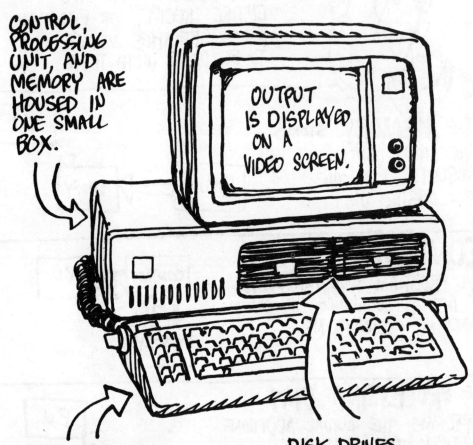

CONTROL, PROCESSING UNIT, AND MEMORY ARE HOUSED IN ONE SMALL BOX.

OUTPUT IS DISPLAYED ON A VIDEO SCREEN.

INPUT IS ENTERED FROM KEYBOARD.

DISK DRIVES PROVIDE EXTRA MEMORY STORAGE

OTHER COMMON INPUT/OUTPUT DEVICES (NOT PICTURED) ARE A **MODEM**, FOR SENDING AND RECEIVING SIGNALS OVER THE PHONE, AND A **PRINTER**, FOR PRODUCING OUTPUT ON PAPER.

LET'S START IN THE MIDDLE, WITH THE

PROCESSING ▮▮▮ ▮▮▮ UNIT ⠿

IN THE KITCHEN, A CHEF MAY DISPLAY A RICH REPERTOIRE OF PROCESSING POSSIBILITIES:

BRAISE
BROIL
SAUTÉ
ROAST
POACH
STEAM
BOIL
FRY
BAKE...

BUT, AS THE GREAT ESCOFFIER HIMSELF HAS REMARKED, ALL COOKING TECHNIQUES ARE COMBINATIONS OF SIMPLER STEPS: THE APPLICATION OF MORE OR LESS HEAT, WET OR DRY, ETC...

THESE FEW ARE ELEMENTARY!

 LIKEWISE, ALL THE POWER OF THE COMPUTER DEPENDS ON A COUPLE OF ELEMENTARY OPERATIONS.

O.K...O.K... NO MORE BEATING AROUND THE BUSH WITH CULINARY METAPHORS...

THE COMPUTER'S ELEMENTARY OPERATIONS ARE

LOGICAL

LOGICAL?

WHAT'S A LOGICAL OPERATION, YOU ASK? A LOGICAL QUESTION, CONSIDERING HOW MUCH EASIER IT IS TO THINK OF ILLOGICAL OPERATIONS, LIKE AMPUTATION OF THE THUMBS OR GETTING OUT OF BED ON MONDAYS...

NOTHING IS LOGICAL ON MONDAYS...

TO EVERYONE'S GOOD FORTUNE, LOGIC ISN'T AS HARD AS IT USED TO BE. IN ARISTOTLE'S TIME, THE SUBJECT WAS DIVIDED INTO INDUCTIVE AND DEDUCTIVE BRANCHES, INDUCTIVE LOGIC BEING THE ART OF INFERRING TRUTHS BY OBSERVING NATURE, WHILE DEDUCTIVE LOGIC DEDUCED TRUTHS FROM OTHER TRUTHS:

DEDUCTIVE↱

1. YOU ARE A MAN.
2. ALL MEN ARE MORTAL.
3. THEREFORE, YOU ARE MORTAL.

INDUCTIVE↴

≶AHEM≶ HOW DO YOU **KNOW** ALL MEN ARE MORTAL??

MEDIEVAL

LOGICIANS COMPOUNDED THE CONFUSION WITH SIX "MODES": A STATEMENT WAS EITHER TRUE, FALSE, NECESSARY, CONTINGENT, POSSIBLE, OR IMPOSSIBLE.

NECESSARY IS TO CONTINGENT AS TRUE IS TO FALSE... POSSIBLY...

THEIR REASONING GREW SO MINDLESS THAT THE MEDIEVAL LOGICIAN **DUNS SCOTUS** HAS BEEN IMMORTALIZED IN THE WORD "DUNCE"!

THE SUBJECT WAS STRETCHED TO ABSURD LENGTHS BY **LEWIS CARROLL**:

"(1) GENTILES HAVE NO OBJECTION TO PORK.

(2) NOBODY WHO ADMIRES PIGSTIES EVER READS HOGG'S POEMS.

(3) NO MANDARIN KNOWS HEBREW.

(4) EVERYONE, WHO DOES NOT OBJECT TO PORK, ADMIRES TURNSTILES.

(5) NO JEW IS IGNORANT OF HEBREW.

THEREFORE, NO MANDARIN EVER READS HOGG'S POEMS. " *

CLEARLY, IT WAS TIME TO SIMPLIFY THE SUBJECT...

* FROM SYMBOLIC LOGIC

THIS STEP WAS TAKEN BY **GEORGE BOOLE** (1815-1864), AN ENGLISH MATHEMATICIAN WHO BUILT AN "ALGEBRA" OUT OF LOGIC.

THAT IS, HE MADE LOGIC FULLY **SYMBOLIC**, JUST LIKE MATH. SENTENCES WERE DENOTED BY LETTERS AND CONNECTED BY ALGEBRAIC SYMBOLS — AN IDEA GOING BACK TO **LEIBNIZ**, WHO HAD DREAMED OF "JUSTICE BY ALGEBRA."

$(1-x)\cdot(1-y) = 1-x-y+xy$. THEREFORE, 30 YEARS!

WE CAN'T POSSIBLY DESCRIBE BOOLE'S ALGEBRA IN ITS ENTIRETY. WE'LL LIMIT OURSELVES TO *THREE WORDS*:

AND, OR, NOT!

BOOLE LOOKED AT THE VERY CONNECTIVE TISSUE OF LANGUAGE: THE WORDS "AND", "OR", AND "NOT".

SUPPOSE P IS ANY STATEMENT... FOR EXAMPLE,

P = "The pig has spots."

ACCORDING TO BOOLE, THIS SENTENCE IS EITHER TRUE (*T*) OR FALSE (*F*). NO OTHER OPTION IS ALLOWED! *

T   F

NOW LET Q BE ANOTHER STATEMENT—LIKEWISE TRUE OR FALSE:

Q = "The pig is glad."

T   F

NOW FORM THE COMPOUND SENTENCES:

P AND Q = THE PIG IS SPOTTED **AND** THE PIG IS GLAD.

P OR Q = THE PIG IS SPOTTED **OR** THE PIG IS GLAD.

WHEN ARE THESE SENTENCES TRUE?   (P OR Q?)

* IN SOME VERSIONS OF LOGIC, MORE THAN TWO TRUTH VALUES ARE PERMISSIBLE.

THERE ARE FOUR POSSIBLE COMBINATIONS OF TRUTH AND FALSEHOOD FOR P AND Q:

 P TRUE, Q TRUE

 P FALSE, Q TRUE

P TRUE, Q FALSE

P FALSE, Q FALSE

AND

"THE PIG IS GLAD **AND** HAS SPOTS."

THIS IS TRUE ONLY IN THE ONE CASE IN WHICH P, Q ARE BOTH TRUE. THIS IS SUMMARIZED IN A *TRUTH TABLE*:

P	Q	P AND Q
T	T	T
T	F	F
F	T	F
F	F	F

OR

" THE PIG IS GLAD **OR** HAS SPOTS."

THIS IS TRUE IN THE THREE CASES FOR WHICH EITHER ONE OF THE STATEMENTS P, Q IS TRUE.

P	Q	P OR Q
T	T	T
T	F	T
F	T	T
F	F	F

AND ONE MORE LOGICAL OPERATOR—

NOT-P = The pig is NOT spotted.

THIS OPERATOR SIMPLY TURNS A STATEMENT INTO ITS OPPOSITE.

P	NOT-P
T	F
F	T

BOOLE MADE THIS LOOK ALGEBRAIC IN SOMETHING LIKE THE FOLLOWING WAY:

☆ DENOTE T BY 1

☆ DENOTE F BY 0

☆ DENOTE AND BY $\cdot$

☆ DENOTE OR BY $\oplus$

☆ DENOTE NOT BY $1-$

MY OWN PRIVATE ALGEBRA!

THEN THE TRUTH TABLES BECOME:

$$1 \cdot 1 = 1 \qquad 1 \oplus 1 = 1 \qquad 1 - 1 = 0$$
$$1 \cdot 0 = 0 \qquad 1 \oplus 0 = 1 \qquad 1 - 0 = 1$$
$$0 \cdot 1 = 0 \qquad 0 \oplus 1 = 1$$
$$0 \cdot 0 = 0 \qquad 0 \oplus 0 = 0$$

EXCEPT FOR THE ONE WEIRD EQUATION $|\oplus| = 1$, THESE LOOK LIKE ORDINARY ARITHMETIC... WITH "AND" PLAYING THE ROLE OF "TIMES" AND "OR" IN THE ROLE OF "PLUS."

AND "NOT" IN THE ROLE OF NON-PLUSED?

WE'RE NEVER GOING TO USE THE SYMBOLS $\cdot$ AND $\oplus$... YOU CAN FORGET ABOUT THEM... BUT USING 1 AND 0 TO REPRESENT TRUE AND FALSE IS VERY USEFUL... SO FROM NOW ON WE'LL WRITE TRUTH TABLES LIKE THIS:

P	Q	P AND Q
1	1	1
1	0	0
0	1	0
0	0	0

P	Q	P OR Q
1	1	1
1	0	1
0	1	1
0	0	0

P	NOT-P
1	0
0	1

FROM THESE RELATIONSHIPS, BOOLE BUILT UP AN ENTIRE ALGEBRA, USING ONLY THE NUMBERS 0 AND 1... TODAY THIS *BOOLEAN ALGEBRA* IS USED ALL THE TIME BY COMPUTER ENGINEERS — ONLY THEY EXPRESS IT AS *ELECTRICAL CIRCUITS*...

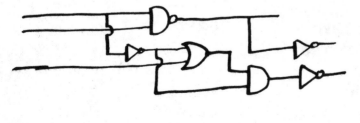

LOGICAL SPAGHETTI!

THE KEY IS THE **AUTOMATIC SWITCH,** WHICH IS EITHER OPEN OR CLOSED, AS A LOGICAL PROPOSITION IS EITHER TRUE OR FALSE.

AN AUTOMATIC SWITCH HAS TWO WIRES COMING IN AND ONE GOING OUT.*

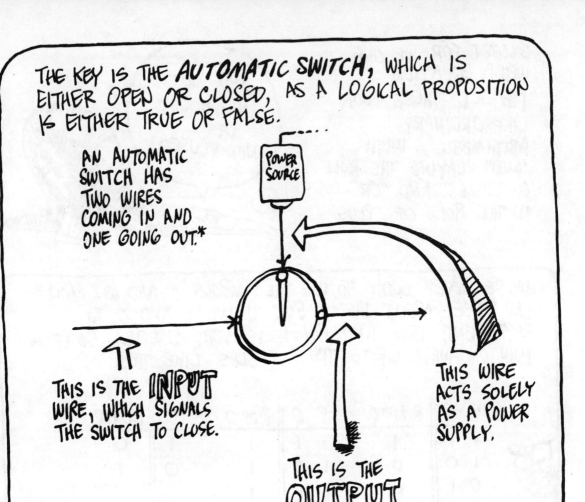

POWER SOURCE

THIS IS THE **INPUT** WIRE, WHICH SIGNALS THE SWITCH TO CLOSE.

THIS IS THE **OUTPUT** WIRE.

THIS WIRE ACTS SOLELY AS A POWER SUPPLY.

*IGNORING THE GROUND WIRE!

WHEN NO CURRENT FLOWS THROUGH THE INPUT WIRE, THE SWITCH REMAINS OPEN, AS PICTURED ABOVE. WHEN AN INPUT SIGNAL ARRIVES, HOWEVER, THE ELECTRONIC EQUIVALENT OF A MINIATURE BOXING GLOVE "PUNCHES" THE SWITCH CLOSED RESULTING IN AN OUTPUT SIGNAL.

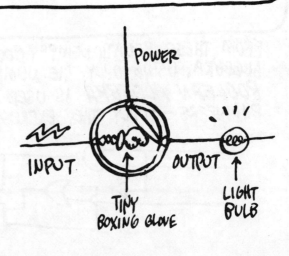

POWER

INPUT

OUTPUT

TINY BOXING GLOVE

LIGHT BULB

WHAT IS THE OUTPUT WHEN TWO SWITCHES (A, B) ARE ARRANGED IN SERIES, ONE AFTER THE OTHER? [IN OUR DIAGRAM, PLEASE NOTE THE REARRANGEMENT OF WIRES, MADE FOR CONVENIENCE OF ILLUSTRATION.]

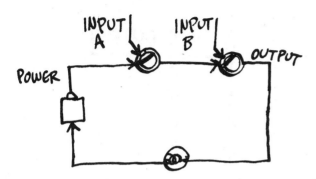

THE CURRENT CAN FLOW ONLY IF *BOTH* SWITCHES ARE CLOSED — I.E., WHEN INPUT SIGNALS ARRIVE SIMULTANEOUSLY AT A AND B.

WRITING 1 FOR CURRENT AND O FOR NO CURRENT, WE CAN THEN WRITE THIS **INPUT-OUTPUT** TABLE. LOOK FAMILIAR? IT SHOULD! IT'S IDENTICAL TO THE TRUTH TABLE FOR *AND*!

A	B	OUTPUT
1	1	1
1	0	0
0	1	0
0	0	0

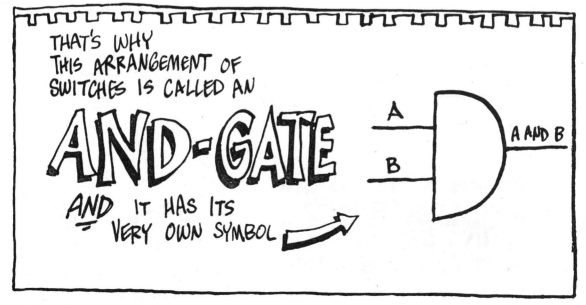

THAT'S WHY THIS ARRANGEMENT OF SWITCHES IS CALLED AN

AND-GATE

AND IT HAS ITS VERY OWN SYMBOL →

A
B
A AND B

TWO SWITCHES CONNECTED IN PARALLEL BEHAVE LIKE LOGICAL **OR** : CURRENT CAN PASS FROM POWER TO OUTPUT IF EITHER SWITCH A, B IS CLOSED (OR IF BOTH ARE).

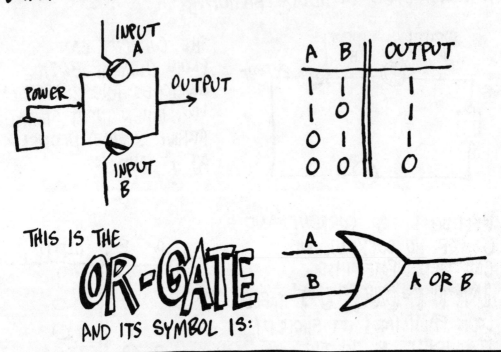

A	B	OUTPUT
1	1	1
1	0	1
0	1	1
0	0	0

THIS IS THE **OR-GATE** AND ITS SYMBOL IS:

NOT IS **NOT** ANY MORE DIFFICULT... IT USES A SPECIAL SWITCH THAT REMAINS CLOSED UNTIL AN INPUT SIGNAL OPENS IT — JUST THE REVERSE OF AN ORDINARY SWITCH :

A	OUTPUT
1	0
0	1

THIS KIND OF SWITCH IS CALLED AN **INVERTER**, AND IT HAS A SYMBOL, TOO:

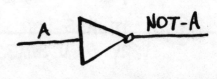

AN EVERYDAY EXAMPLE SHOWS HOW THESE SIMPLE GATES CAN MAKE LOGICAL DECISIONS.

YOU KNOW THOSE BUZZERS THAT GO OFF WHEN YOU START YOUR CAR AND YOUR SEAT BELT ISN'T FASTENED? THE KIND THAT'S SPECIALLY DESIGNED TO PENETRATE HUMAN BONE?

WELL, THAT'S BECAUSE THE SEAT BELT AND IGNITION ARE CONNECTED BY AN **AND-GATE**, LIKE SO:

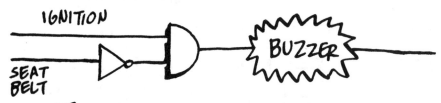

IGNITION

SEAT BELT

BUZZER

THAT IS, **IF** THE IGNITION IS ON **AND** THE SEAT BELT IS **NOT**, THE BUZZER SOUNDS! PRETTY LOGICAL, NO?

CAN YOU THINK OF ANY EXAMPLES OF OR-GATES IN DAILY LIFE?

NOT AT THE MOMENT... I'M BUSY!

(HOW ABOUT A SMOKE ALARM TRIGGERED BY EITHER OF TWO DIFFERENT DETECTORS?)

HERE ARE A FEW WARM-UP EXERCISES FOR CHASING THROUGH LOGIC DIAGRAMS:

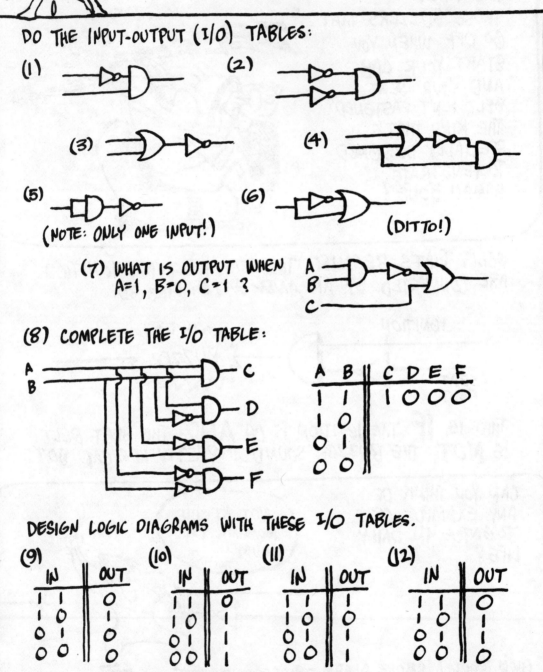

DO THE INPUT-OUTPUT (I/O) TABLES:

(1)

(2)

(3)

(4)

(5)

(NOTE: ONLY ONE INPUT!)

(6)

(DITTO!)

(7) WHAT IS OUTPUT WHEN A=1, B=0, C=1 ?

A
B
C

(8) COMPLETE THE I/O TABLE:

A
B

C
D
E
F

A	B	C	D	E	F
1	1	1	0	0	0
1	0				
0	1				
0	0				

DESIGN LOGIC DIAGRAMS WITH THESE I/O TABLES.

(9)

IN		OUT
1	1	0
1	0	0
0	1	0
0	0	0

(10)

IN		OUT
1	1	0
1	0	1
0	1	0
0	0	0

(11)

IN		OUT
1	1	1
1	0	0
0	1	0
0	0	1

(12)

IN		OUT
1	1	0
1	0	1
0	1	1
0	0	0

LOGIC GATES HAVE ONLY ONE OR TWO INPUTS AND A SINGLE OUTPUT — BUT COMPUTER COMPONENTS HAVE MANY INPUTS AND OUTPUTS WITH COMPLICATED INPUT/OUTPUT BEHAVIOR:

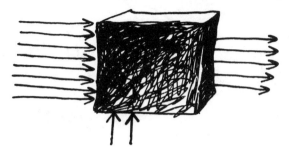

THE WONDERFUL FACT IS THAT **ANY** INPUT/OUTPUT TABLE CAN BE PRODUCED BY A COMBINATION OF LOGIC GATES!

TO DO IT, YOU NEED MULTIPLE-INPUT LOGIC GATES. HERE'S A 4-INPUT **AND**-GATE:

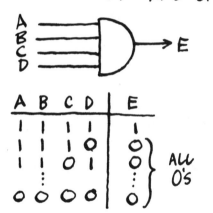

A	B	C	D	E
1	1	1	1	1
1	1	1	0	0
1	1	0	1	0
⋮	⋮	⋮	⋮	⋮
0	0	0	0	0

ALL O'S

THIS MEANS E=1 IF A=B=C=D=1 AND E=O OTHERWISE. THE GATE CAN BE MADE WITH FOUR SWITCHES IN SERIES:

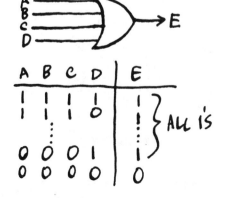

SIMILARLY, THERE'S A MULTIPLE-INPUT **OR**-GATE:

A	B	C	D	E
1	1	1	1	1
1	1	1	0	1
⋮	⋮	⋮	⋮	⋮
0	0	0	1	1
0	0	0	0	0

ALL 1'S

IT CAN ACTUALLY BE MADE FROM AN **AND**-GATE AND SOME INVERTERS:

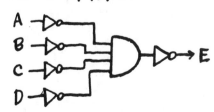

AS AN EXAMPLE OF HOW TO PRODUCE A GIVEN INPUT/OUTPUT
TABLE, LET'S SOLVE PROBLEM #12:

IN		OUT
A	B	C
1	1	0
1	0	1
0	1	1
0	0	0

BEGIN BY
FINDING ALL ROWS
WHERE C=1.

THE TABLE SAYS C=1 IF A=1 AND B=0 OR A=0 AND B=1.
C=0 OTHERWISE.

WRITING $\bar{A}$ FOR NOT-A, THIS AMOUNTS TO SAYING

C=1 IF A=1 AND $\bar{B}$=1 OR $\bar{A}$=1 AND B=1.
C=0 OTHERWISE.

IN OTHER WORDS,

$$C = (A \text{ AND } \bar{B}) \text{ OR } (\bar{A} \text{ AND } B)$$

TO DRAW THE CIRCUIT, RUN THE INPUT WIRES AND THEIR
NEGATIVES IN ONE DIRECTION —

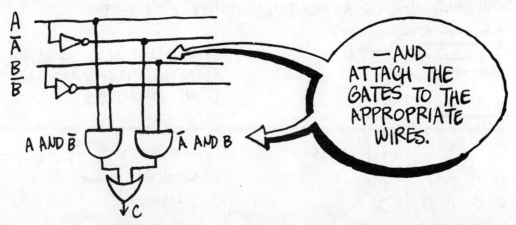

—AND
ATTACH THE
GATES TO THE
APPROPRIATE
WIRES.

EXACTLY THE SAME METHOD WORKS FOR MORE INPUTS. FOR EXAMPLE:

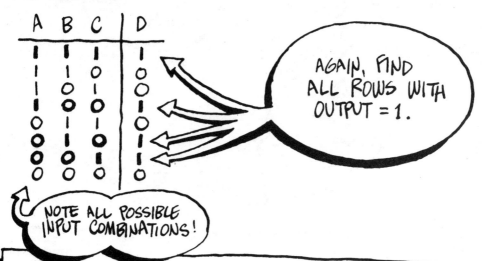

A	B	C	D
1	1	1	1
1	1	0	0
1	0	1	0
1	0	0	1
0	1	1	0
0	1	0	1
0	0	1	1
0	0	0	0

AGAIN, FIND ALL ROWS WITH OUTPUT = 1.

NOTE ALL POSSIBLE INPUT COMBINATIONS!

IN THIS CASE,

$$D = (A \text{ AND } B \text{ AND } C) \text{ OR } (A \text{ AND } \bar{B} \text{ AND } \bar{C}) \text{ OR } (\bar{A} \text{ AND } B \text{ AND } \bar{C}) \text{ OR } (\bar{A} \text{ AND } \bar{B} \text{ AND } C).$$

RUN THE INPUTS AND THEIR NEGATIVES ACROSS THE PAGE, ATTACH AND-GATES, THEN RUN THEM THROUGH AN OR-GATE!

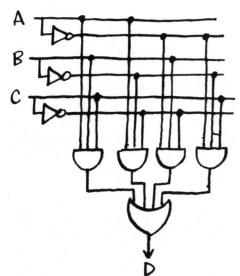

TO REPEAT: BY THE SAME METHOD, YOU CAN PRODUCE ANY INPUT/OUTPUT TABLE!!

WHERE DOES THIS LEAVE US?

WITH ONE FOOT IN THE SWAMP!

IGNORANCE.

BY NOW YOU MAY BE GETTING THE IDEA THAT INFORMATION IS ENCODED INSIDE COMPUTERS AS STRINGS OF 1's AND 0's, WHICH CAN BE TRANSFORMED IN ANY WAY WE LIKE BY THE RIGHT COMBINATION OF LOGIC GATES.

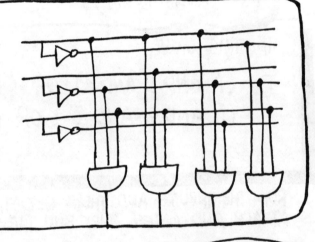

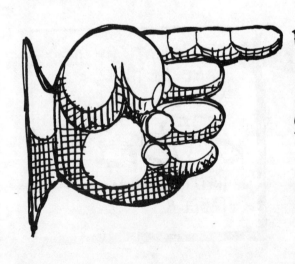

BUT WE HAVEN'T REALLY SEEN HOW LOGIC GATES CAN DO THE JOB COMPUTERS WERE DESIGNED FOR:

NAMELY: HOW DO COMPUTERS COMPUTE?

The questions:

☐ IS THERE SOME NATURAL WAY TO REPRESENT NUMBERS USING ONLY 0's AND 1's? CAN THE OPERATIONS OF ARITHMETIC BE BUILT OUT OF LOGIC?

The answer

(WHICH GOES BACK TO OUR OLD PAL LEIBNIZ):

AS SURE AS I DIDN'T STEAL CALCULUS FROM NEWTON!

THE SYSTEM IS CALLED

BINARY NUMBERS.

THEY'RE BASED ON *TWO!*

OUR DECIMAL SYSTEM, BASED ON TEN, WAS A RESULT OF OUR HAVING TEN FINGERS — AN ACCIDENT OF NATURE! BINARY NUMBERS ARE WHAT WOULD HAVE EVOLVED IF WE'D BEEN BORN WITH *TWO* FINGERS, LIKE THE TREE SLOTH.

I'D COUNT BY FOURS, BUT I ONLY HAVE ONE FREE PAW!

TREE SLOTHS ALWAYS COUNT IN BINARY!

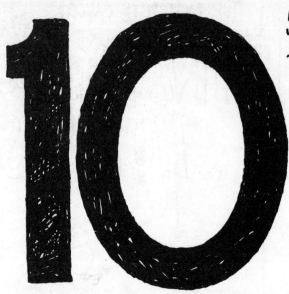 LOOK AT THE SYMBOL "10" — "ONE-ZERO." FORGET THAT IT USUALLY MEANS TEN! FORGET IT! STOP CALLING IT THAT! IS THERE ANYTHING THERE THAT SAYS "TEN?" **NO!!** IT'S JUST A ONE FOLLOWED BY A ZERO — IN AND OF ITSELF, IT HAS **NOTHING TO DO** WITH TEN!!!

THE SYMBOL ONLY MAKES "TEN" FLASH THROUGH YOUR MIND BECAUSE YOU'VE ALWAYS CALLED IT THAT... IT'S LIKE A RITUAL: PERFORM IT OVER AND OVER AND IT BECOMES AUTOMATIC!

IN ACTUALITY, "10" MEANS:

 **I** (ONE) HANDFUL* AND

O (ZERO) FINGERS LEFT OVER

*REMEMBER — ON P. 24, WE AGREED TO CALL TEN FINGERS, NOT FIVE, A HUMAN HANDFUL!

116

SINCE WE HUMANS HAVE TEN FINGERS, OUR "10" IS TEN... BUT TO AN ORGANISM WITH, SAY, EIGHT FINGERS, 10 WOULD MEAN EIGHT!

IN THE CASE AT HAND, WITH JUST TWO FINGERS IN A HANDFUL... 10 MEANS **TWO!!**

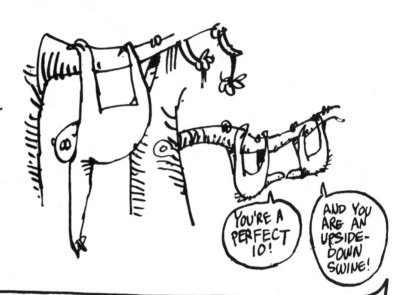

YOU'RE A PERFECT 10!

AND YOU ARE AN UPSIDE-DOWN SWINE!

SO WE CAN WRITE?

$$10_{\text{BINARY}} = 2_{\text{DECIMAL}}$$

NOTE: DO **NOT** READ THIS AS "TEN EQUALS TWO." TEN DOES NOT EQUAL TWO!! "ONE-ZERO IN BINARY" EQUALS TWO!!

TWO TWO TWO TWO

TWO TWO TWO

TWO TWO TWO

LIKEWISE, **100** — "ONE-ZERO-ZERO" — MEANS

1 HANDFUL OF HANDFULS.

IN DECIMAL, THAT'S 10×10, OR A HUNDRED. WELL, IN BINARY IT'S 10×10 ALSO — BUT THAT ONLY AMOUNTS TO *FOUR!*

1000 IS

$$10 \times 10 \times 10 = 2 \times 2 \times 2 = 8$$
$$\vdots$$

AND GENERALLY,

1 FOLLOWED BY N ZEROES IS:

$$\underbrace{2 \times \cdots \times 2}_{N \text{ TIMES}} = 2^N$$

("TWO TO THE N^{TH} POWER").

IN THE COMPUTER AGE, EVERYONE WILL BE REQUIRED BY LAW TO MEMORIZE THE POWERS OF TWO, UP TO 2^{10}. BETTER NOT WAIT! AVOID JAIL AND DO IT NOW!

$$1 = 2^0 = 1$$
$$10 = 2^1 = 2$$
$$100 = 2^2 = 4$$
$$1000 = 2^3 = 8$$
$$10000 = 2^4 = 16$$
$$100000 = 2^5 = 32$$
$$1000000 = 2^6 = 64$$
$$10000000 = 2^7 = 128$$
$$100000000 = 2^8 = 256$$
$$1000000000 = 2^9 = 512$$
$$10000000000 = 2^{10} = 1024$$

AND 10101110?

ALL OTHER BINARY NUMBERS — 101, 1111, 11000, AND EVERY OTHER PATTERN OF 0's AND 1's — IS A SUM OF SUCH POWERS OF TWO! IT'S COMPLETELY ANALOGOUS TO DECIMAL.

IN DECIMAL:

$$497 =$$

$$400$$
$$+\ 90$$
$$+\ \ \ 7$$

IN BINARY:

$$111110001 =$$

100000000	256
+ 10000000	128
+ 1000000	64
+ 100000	32
+ 10000	16
+ 1	1
	497

TO TRANSLATE A BINARY NUMBER INTO THE DECIMAL SYSTEM, LIST THE POWERS OF TWO OVER THE CORRESPONDING PLACES, AND ADD THOSE LYING OVER A 1.

$$\cdots\ 2^{10}\ 2^{9}\ 2^{8}\ 2^{7}\ 2^{6}\ 2^{5}\ 2^{4}\ 2^{3}\ 2^{2}\ 2^{1}$$
$$1\ \ 0\ \ 0\ \ 0\ \ 1\ \ 1\ \ 0\ \ 1\ \ 0$$

$$256\ \ +\ \ 16+8+2\ \ = 282$$

NOW YOU DO IT. CONVERT TO DECIMAL:

(1) 11   (2) 101   (3) 11111111   (4) 110101010111101

TO MAKE THIS A BIT MORE CONCRETE — HERE'S HOW TO COUNT UP FROM 1 IN BINARY. IT'S JUST LIKE COUNTING IN DECIMAL, ONLY EASIER. IN DECIMAL, TO COUNT PAST A 9, YOU WRITE 0 AND CARRY 1. IN BINARY, YOU HAVE TO CARRY 1 EVERY OTHER NUMBER!!

EASY AS FALLING OUT OF BED!

BINARY	DECIMAL
0	0
1	1
10	2
11	3
100	4
101	5
110	6
111	7
1000	8
1001	9
1010	10
1011	11
1100	12
1101	13
1110	14
1111	15
10000	16
10001	17
10010	18
10011	19
10100	20
⋮	⋮
ETC!	ETC!

AS YOU MAY HAVE NOTICED, BINARY NUMBERS GET **LONNNNNNG** VERY FAST!

THIS MAKES THEM HARD FOR US HUMANS TO USE WITHOUT MAKING MISTAKES — BUT FOR COMPUTERS THEY'RE IDEAL!!

BINARY CALCULATION IS SIMPLE. THERE ARE ONLY FIVE RULES TO REMEMBER:

$$0 + 0 = 0$$

$$0 + 1 = 1$$

$$1 + 0 = 1$$

$$1 + 1 = 10$$

AND THE HANDY FIFTH RULE:

$$1 + 1 + 1 = 11$$

AS OPPOSED TO 100 SUMS IN DECIMAL: 9+6, 7+5, 9+3, 8+4, 4+6, ETC ETC ETC !!!

TO ADD TWO BINARY NUMBERS, PROCEED PLACE BY PLACE FROM RIGHT TO LEFT, CARRYING A 1 WHEN NECESSARY. HERE'S A STEP-BY-STEP EXAMPLE:

```
   1110        1110       1110       1110
 +  111      +  111     +  111     +  111
 ------      ------     ------     ------
      1          01        101      10101
```

THE CARRIES

. . . .

A FEW SUMS TO PRACTICE ON:

```
  100      11      11001      11011      1111111111
+   1    +  1    + 1100     +11011     +1111111111
```

➡ WHAT IS THE RESULT OF ADDING A BINARY NUMBER TO ITSELF?

ANOTHER WONDERFUL FACT ABOUT BINARY:

SUBTRACTION IS DONE BY ADDING !!

THE METHOD IS CALLED USING "TWO'S COMPLEMENT." FIRST YOU INVERT THE NUMBER TO BE SUBTRACTED, SO THAT ALL ITS 1's BECOME 0's AND VICE VERSA. THEN ADD THE TWO NUMBERS AND ADD 1 TO THE SUM. IGNORE THE FINAL CARRY AND THAT'S THE ANSWER!

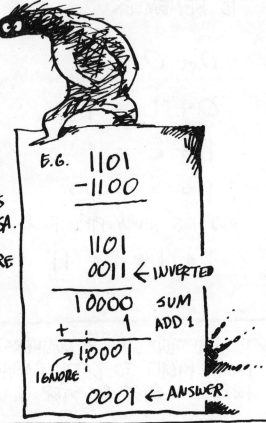

E.G.
```
   1101
  -1100
  _____

   1101
   0011  ← INVERTED
  _____
  10000    SUM
 +    1    ADD 1
  _____
  1:0001
 IGNORE

  0001  ← ANSWER.
```

BINARY MULTIPLICATION — AND ANY MULTIPLICATION — MAY ALSO BE DONE BY REPEATED ADDITION: TO MULTIPLY A × B, JUST ADD A TO ITSELF B TIMES. LIKEWISE, DIVISION CAN BE DONE BY REPEATED SUBTRACTION.

```
 110 × 11 =

    110  ⎫
  + 110  ⎬ 11 TIMES
  + 110  ⎭
  _____
  10010
```

The computer can do all arithmetic by adding !!

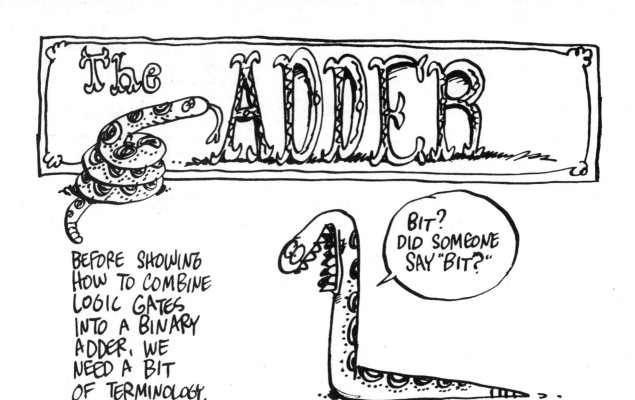

The ADDER

BEFORE SHOWING HOW TO COMBINE LOGIC GATES INTO A BINARY ADDER, WE NEED A BIT OF TERMINOLOGY.

BIT? DID SOMEONE SAY "BIT?"

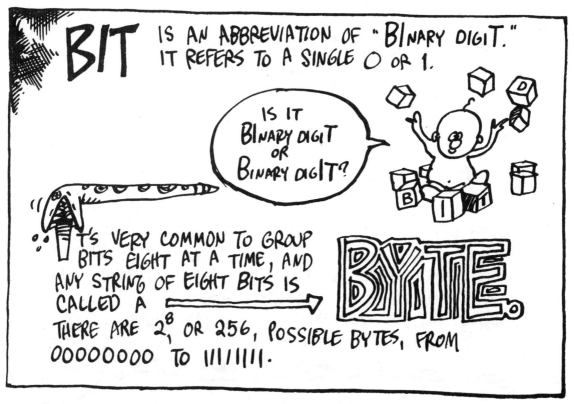

BIT IS AN ABBREVIATION OF "BINARY DIGIT." IT REFERS TO A SINGLE 0 OR 1.

IS IT BINARY digit OR BINARY digIT?

IT'S VERY COMMON TO GROUP BITS EIGHT AT A TIME, AND ANY STRING OF EIGHT BITS IS CALLED A ⟶ **BYTE.**

THERE ARE 2^8, OR 256, POSSIBLE BYTES, FROM 00000000 TO 11111111.

NOW LET'S SEE WHAT AN ADDER MIGHT LOOK LIKE.

THIS ADDER LOOKS LIKE A POISONOUS NOSE...

TO SAVE DRAWING, WE'LL MAKE IT A FOUR-BIT ADDER, CAPABLE OF ADDING TWO 4-BIT NUMBERS, OR "NIBBLES" (YES, THEY'RE REALLY CALLED THAT!)

$$A = 1110$$
$$B = \underline{1011}$$
$$11001$$

THE **INPUT** OF OUR ADDER MUST CONSIST OF EIGHT BITS, FOUR FOR EACH NIBBLE. THE **OUTPUT** MUST BE FIVE BITS, THAT IS, A NIBBLE PLUS ONE BIT FOR A POSSIBLE CARRY. LIKE SO:

A

B

A+B

ANY NUMBER FROM ZERO TO FIFTEEN

ANY NUMBER FROM ZERO TO THIRTY

HOW TO PROCEED? ONE WAY IS TO MAKE A GIANT TRUTH TABLE, MATCHING EVERY POSSIBLE COMBINATION OF INPUTS WITH THE CORRECT OUTPUT, AND CONSTRUCTING A HUGE STEW OF ANDs AND NOTs TO FORCE A SOLUTION. THIS IS POSSIBLE, BUT THE COMPLEXITY OF THE TASK MIGHT MAKE YOU THROW UP YOUR HANDS.

OR JUST THROW UP, IF YOU HAVE NO HANDS!

INSTEAD, RECALL HOW ADDITION WORKS IN PRACTICE: COLUMN BY COLUMN, WITH A **CARRY BIT** CARRYING OUT OF ONE COLUMN AND INTO THE NEXT:

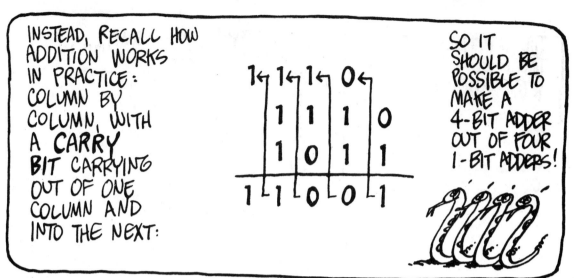

SO IT SHOULD BE POSSIBLE TO MAKE A 4-BIT ADDER OUT OF FOUR 1-BIT ADDERS!

THE 1-BIT ADDER MUST HAVE THREE INPUTS — ONE FOR EACH OF THE TWO SUMMAND BITS AND ONE FOR THE BIT CARRIED IN — AND TWO OUTPUTS — ONE SUM BIT AND ONE CARRY-OUT BIT.

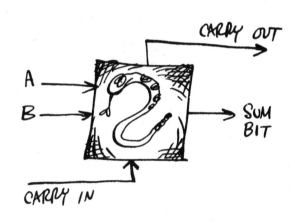

CARRY OUT

A

B

SUM BIT

CARRY IN

FOUR OF THESE CAN THEN BE HOOKED UP TO PRODUCE A 4-BIT ADDER:

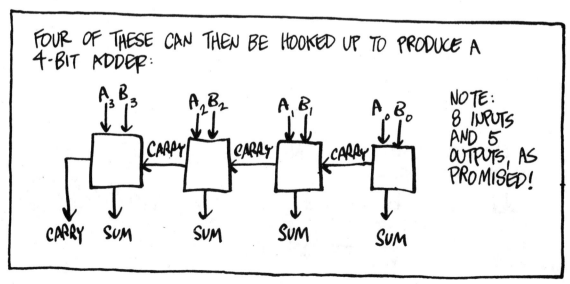

A_3 B_3 A_2 B_2 A_1 B_1 A_0 B_0

CARRY   CARRY   CARRY

CARRY   SUM   SUM   SUM   SUM

NOTE: 8 INPUTS AND 5 OUTPUTS, AS PROMISED!

THE INPUT/OUTPUT
TABLE FOR THE
1-BIT ADDER:

A	B	CARRY IN	CARRY OUT	SUM BIT
1	1	0	1	0
1	0	1	1	0
1	0	0	1	0
0	1	1	1	0
0	1	0	0	1
0	0	1	0	1
0	0	0	0	0

NOW THERE'S NOTHING TO IT! REMEMBER, LOGIC GATES CAN BE RIGGED UP TO PRODUCE ANY INPUT/OUTPUT TABLE. IN THIS CASE, JUST TREAT EACH OUTPUT COLUMN SEPARATELY:

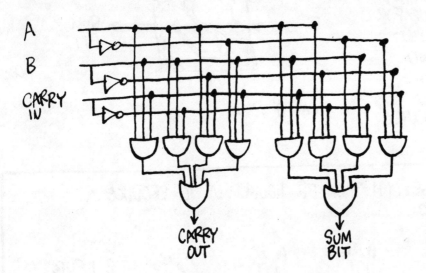

YOU CAN ADD TWO NUMBERS OF ANY LENGTH BY HOOKING TOGETHER ENOUGH 1-BIT ADDERS.

CODING & COMBINATION

BINARY TASTES RIGHT!

THE IMPLICATION OF THE LAST TWO SECTIONS IS THAT BINARY IS THE "NATURAL" SYSTEM FOR ENCODING NUMBERS IN A MACHINE MADE OF ON/OFF SWITCHES. EVEN SO, COMPUTERS USE SEVERAL VARIATIONS ON THE BASIC IDEA.

INTEGERS, OR WHOLE NUMBERS — IF THEY AREN'T TOO LARGE — ARE ENCODED IN STRAIGHT BINARY. FOR INSTANCE,

185

WOULD BECOME

1	0	1	1	1	0	0	1

FLOATING POINT REPRESENTATION IS FOR LARGE OR FRACTIONAL NUMBERS. FOR EXAMPLE, 19,700,030.2 WOULD BE ENCODED AS THE BINARY EQUIVALENT OF

197	5

MEANING 197×10^5.

FLOATING POINT REPRESENTATION OFTEN INVOLVES ROUNDING OFF.

BINARY CODED DECIMAL REPRESENTS A NUMBER IN DECIMAL, BUT WITH EACH DIGIT ENCODED IN BINARY. 967, FOR INSTANCE, WOULD BECOME

1001   0110   0111

9   6   7

AND WHAT ABOUT *NON*-NUMERICAL INFORMATION — THE ALPHABET, PUNCTUATION MARKS, OTHER SYMBOLS, AND EVEN THE BLANK SPACE ??

SINCE THERE IS NO NATURAL WAY TO ENCODE THESE INTO 0'S AND 1'S, COMPUTER SCIENTISTS INVENTED AND ADOPTED A STANDARD CODE BY MUTUAL AGREEMENT:

ASCII,

THE AMERICAN STANDARD CODE FOR INFORMATION INTERCHANGE.

(ACTUALLY, ASCII IS USED BY EVERYONE BUT IBM, WHICH HAS ITS OWN CODE, CALLED EBCDIC.)

UNITY! WHERE IS UNITY?

NEXT FOUR BITS	000	001	010	011	100	101	110	111
0000	NUL	DLE	SP	0	@	P	`	p
0001	SOH	DC1	!	1	A	Q	a	q
0010	STX	DC2	"	2	B	R	b	r
0011	ETX	DC3	#	3	C	S	c	s
0100	EOT	DC4	$	4	D	T	d	t
0101	ENQ	NAK	%	5	E	U	e	u
0110	ACK	SYN	&	6	F	V	f	v
0111	BEL	ETB	'	7	G	W	g	w
1000	BS	CAN	(	8	H	X	h	x
1001	HT	EM	)	9	I	Y	i	y
1010	LF	SUB	*	:	J	Z	j	z
1011	VT	ESC	+	;	K	[	k	{
1100	FF	FS	,	<	L	\	l		
1101	CR	GS	-	=	M	]	m	}
1110	SO	RS	.	>	N	^	n	~
1111	SI	US	/	?	O	—	o	DEL

FIRST THREE BITS (column header)

☆ THUS, THE LETTER "T" IS ENCODED AS 101 0100... ETC!

☆ THE FIRST TWO COLUMNS CONTAIN SYMBOLS FOR SUCH THINGS AS "START OF HEADING" (SOH) AND OTHER TEXTUAL DIRECTIONS.

TO ENCODE AND DECODE DATA, COMPUTERS USE LOGIC DEVICES CALLED, NATURALLY ENOUGH, **ENCODERS** AND **DECODERS**.

AN ENCODER

USUALLY HAS MANY INPUTS AND A FEW OUTPUTS. A SINGLE INPUT SIGNAL PRODUCES A PATTERN OF OUTPUTS. FOR EXAMPLE, A COMPUTER KEYBOARD IS ATTACHED TO AN ENCODER WHICH TRANSLATES A SINGLE KEYSTROKE INTO ITS ASCII CODE.

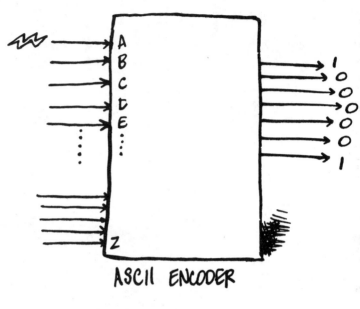

ASCII ENCODER

A DECODER

WORKS THE OTHER WAY AROUND, TRANSLATING A PATTERN OF BITS INTO A SINGLE OUTPUT SIGNAL. ONE DECODER CONVERTS A BINARY NIBBLE INTO A DECIMAL DIGIT. ANOTHER TRANSFORMS A SPECIFIED LOCATION, OR **ADDRESS**, IN MEMORY INTO A SIGNAL TO THAT MEMORY CELL. (SEE P. 155.)

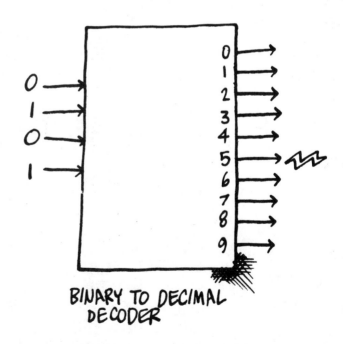

BINARY TO DECIMAL DECODER

ONCE ALPHANUMERIC INFORMATION IS ENCODED IN BINARY STRINGS, IT IS READY TO BE PROCESSED BY THE COMPUTER'S MOST ELABORATE COMBINATION OF LOGIC GATES, THE

ARITHMETIC LOGIC UNIT (OR **ALU**, FOR SHORT).

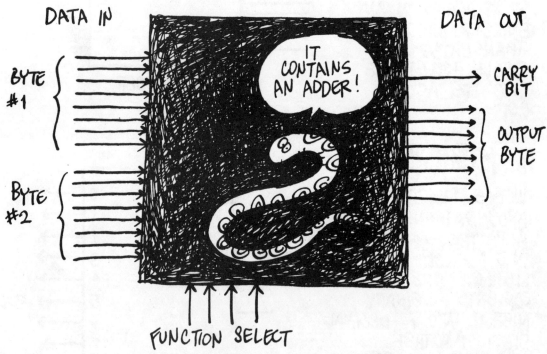

DATA IN

DATA OUT

BYTE #1

BYTE #2

IT CONTAINS AN ADDER!

CARRY BIT

OUTPUT BYTE

FUNCTION SELECT

THIS IS THE MACHINE'S CENTRAL PROCESSOR, WHICH CAN ADD, SUBTRACT, MULTIPLY, COMPARE, SHIFT, AND PERFORM A WEALTH OF OTHER LOGICAL FUNCTIONS. THE DRAWING ABOVE REPRESENTS AN 8-BIT ALU, BUT THEY CAN RANGE FROM FOUR TO SIXTY BIT CAPABILITY, DEPENDING ON THE COMPUTER.

THE *FUNCTION SELECT* INPUTS DETERMINE WHICH ARITHMETIC OR LOGICAL FUNCTION THE ALU IS TO PERFORM, EACH FUNCTION HAVING ITS OWN BINARY CODE. FOR EXAMPLE, *0001* APPLIED TO FUNCTION SELECT MIGHT MEAN **ADD**, IN WHICH CASE ⟶

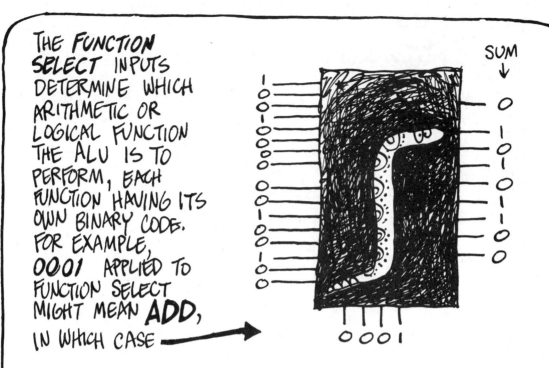

ANOTHER FUNCTION (0101, SAY) MIGHT **COMPARE** TWO BYTES, BIT BY BIT, AND OUTPUT A 1 WHEREVER THEY AGREE. (MEANWHILE, THE ADDER TAKES A NAP.)

YOU CAN GET AN IDEA OF A FANCY ALU'S CAPABILITIES FROM THE LIST ON PAGE 182.

THE ALU WOULD BE A COMPLETE CENTRAL PROCESSING UNIT, EXCEPT FOR ONE THING: IT'S UNABLE TO **STORE** RESULTS. RETURNING TO THE COOKING ANALOGY, WE MIGHT SAY THE ALU LACKS "COUNTER SPACE." WHERE WOULD GRANDMA BABBAGE BE WITHOUT SOMEPLACE TO SET DOWN HER SPAGHETTI?

ALTHOUGH THE ALU CAN PERFORM MIRACLES OF INPUT/OUTPUT, IT CAN'T **REMEMBER** ANYTHING — AND THAT'S WHERE **FLIP-FLOPS** COME IN...

FLIP-FLOPS

LATCH ONTO THIS!

VERSATILE AS THEY MAY BE, THE LOGICAL COMBINATIONS WE'VE BEEN SKETCHING STILL HAVE NO MEMORY. THEIR OUTPUT CONTINUES ONLY AS LONG AS THE INPUT IS APPLIED.

I CAN'T REMEMBER A THING!

HUH?

ME EITHER— HOW ABOUT YOU?

WHA—?

AND YET — THERE IS A WAY TO HOOK THESE LOGICAL BUT SENILE GATES TOGETHER INTO A GADGET THAT *HOLDS* AN OUTPUT INDEFINITELY: THE *FLIP-FLOP.* STARE AT THIS A MINUTE !!

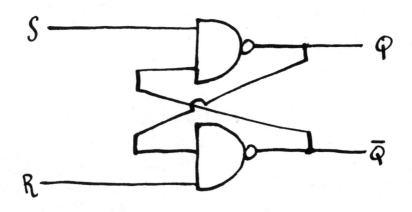

BESIDES THE STRANGE WAY A FLIP-FLOP EATS ITS OWN TAIL, PLEASE NOTE THE UNFAMILIAR GATE USED IN THE CONSTRUCTION. IT'S CALLED A

NAND GATE,

WHICH IS MERELY AN ABBREVIATION OF "NOT-AND."

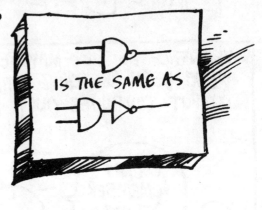

IS THE SAME AS

A	B	NAND
1	1	0
1	0	1
0	1	1
0	0	1

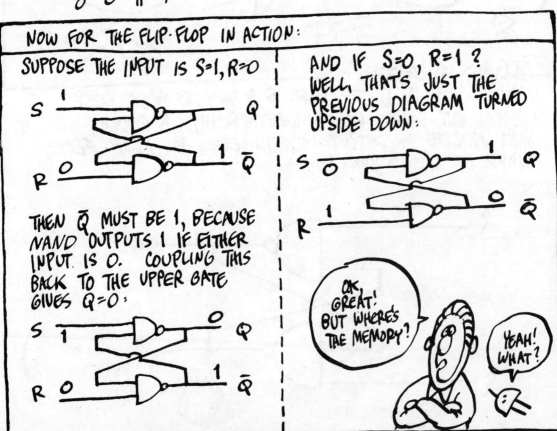

NOW FOR THE FLIP-FLOP IN ACTION:

SUPPOSE THE INPUT IS S=1, R=0

S 1 ———— Q

R 0 ———— 1 Q̄

THEN Q̄ MUST BE 1, BECAUSE NAND OUTPUTS 1 IF EITHER INPUT IS 0. COUPLING THIS BACK TO THE UPPER GATE GIVES Q=0:

S 1 ———— 0 Q

R 0 ———— 1 Q̄

AND IF S=0, R=1? WELL, THAT'S JUST THE PREVIOUS DIAGRAM TURNED UPSIDE DOWN:

S 0 ———— 1 Q

R 1 ———— 0 Q̄

OK, GREAT! BUT WHERE'S THE MEMORY?

YEAH! WHAT?

NOW WHAT HAPPENS
WHEN THE INPUT
CHANGES?
SUPPOSING WE BEGIN WITH
THE INPUT (S=1, R=0),
WHAT DOES CHANGING
IT TO (S=1, R=1)
DO TO THE FLIP-FLOP'S
OUTPUT?

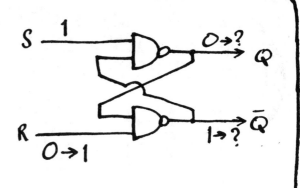

THE ANSWER IS: NOTHING! THE LOWER
NAND-GATE'S INPUT BECOMES (0, 1), SO ITS
OUTPUT $\bar{Q}$ IS STILL 1, SO Q REMAINS 0.

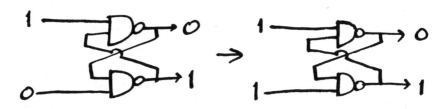

BUT PRECISELY THE SAME LINE OF REASONING SHOWS NO CHANGE
IN OUTPUT WHEN INPUT CHANGES TO (S=1, R=1) FROM
(S=0, R=1):

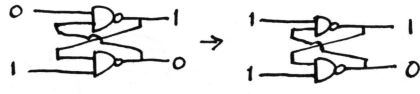

A LITTLE WEIRD, ISN'T IT?
THE SAME INPUT (S=R=1) CAN
PRODUCE TWO DIFFERENT
OUTPUTS, DEPENDING ON THE
PREVIOUS INPUT!

THE
FLIP-FLOP
REMEMBERS!

THE WAY A FLIP-FLOP IS USED IS THIS: IT BEGINS BY SITTING THERE WITH A CONSTANT INPUT OF (S=1, R=1) AND AN OUTPUT OF GOD-KNOWS-WHAT:

YOU **SET** THE FLIP-FLOP [I.E., MAKE Q=1] BY FLASHING A 0 MOMENTARILY DOWN THE S-WIRE, AND THEN RETURNING IT TO 1:

OR YOU CAN **RESET** IT [MAKE Q=0] BY FLASHING A 0 DOWN THE R-WIRE, THEN RETURNING IT TO 1:

IN EITHER CASE, AS LONG AS (1,1) KEEPS COMING IN, THE FLIP-FLOP WILL MAINTAIN ITS OUTPUT UNTIL IT'S CHANGED WITH ANOTHER INCOMING 0.

THE ONLY INPUT COMBINATION WE HAVEN'T CHECKED IS (R=S=0).
IT'S EASY TO VERIFY THAT IT PRODUCES OUTPUT OF Q=Q̄=1 :

WHAT HAPPENS
WHEN THE
INPUT RETURNS
TO (1,1) ?

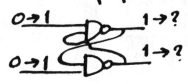

THE ANSWER IS NOT SO CLEAR: IT DEPENDS ON WHICH OUTPUT
HAPPENS TO FLOP FIRST !! (ONE OF THEM MUST.)

IF Q̄ IS FIRST TO
CHANGE, WE GET:

IF Q FLOPS FIRST,
HOWEVER:

SINCE THERE IS **NO WAY** OF KNOWING WHICH OF THESE
WILL ACTUALLY HAPPEN, AND WE DON'T WANT OUR
FLIP-FLOPS IN RANDOM STATES, THE INPUT (S=0, R=0) IS

 # DISALLOWED.

WE CAN SUMMARIZE THE BASIC "R-S" FLIP-FLOP LIKE SO:

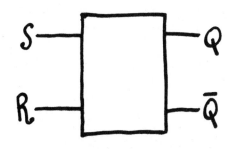

S	R	Q	Q̄
1	1	NO CHANGE	
1	0	0	1
0	1	1	0
0	0	DISALLOWED!	

FLIP-FLOP INPUTS ARE ALWAYS ARRANGED TO MAKE CERTAIN
THE DISALLOWED STATE CANNOT ARRIVE.

GAAAH!

A LITTLE **EXERCISE:**

HVALP!

A *NOR·GATE* IS A SHORTHAND WAY OF WRITING "NOT OR:" I.E.

I AM THE TRUTH!

A	B	NOR
1	1	0
1	0	0
0	1	0
0	0	1

A BASIC R·S FLIP·FLOP MAY ALSO BE MADE OUT OF NOR·GATES:

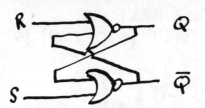

R _____ Q

S _____ $\overline{Q}$

HIYUP!

1. WHAT IS THE OUTPUT WHEN R=0, S=1 ? WHEN S=0, R=1 ?

2. WHAT HAPPENS WHEN EACH OF THESE INPUT CONDITIONS CHANGES TO R=0, S=0 ?

3. WHAT IS THE OUTPUT WHEN R=1, S=1 ? WHAT HAPPENS WHEN THIS CHANGES TO R=0, S=0 ?

4. WHAT INPUT COMBINATION MUST BE DISALLOWED?

5. IF R=0, S=0, HOW DO YOU SET THIS FLIP·FLOP (I.E., MAKE Q=1) ? HOW DO YOU RESET IT ?

BY THE WAY, A FLIP·FLOP IS ALSO CALLED A **LATCH**, BECAUSE IT "LOCKS IN" DATA.

BLEEACH!

138

REGISTERS, COUNTERS, & GLITCHES

IF THE FLIP-FLOP IS A DEVICE FOR STORING ONE BIT, A **REGISTER** STORES SEVERAL BITS SIMULTANEOUSLY. IT'S LIKE A ROW OF BOXES, EACH HOLDING ONE BIT.

A ROW OF FLIP-FLOPS SHOULD DO THE JOB:....

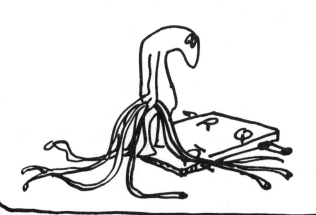

...SORT OF! **BUT** IF YOU TRY AND MAKE THIS WORK BY HOOKING UP SOME INPUTS TO RS FLIP-FLOPS, YOU MAY FIND YOURSELF GROWING CONFUSED!

THE SOLUTION IS TO ADD A "GATING NETWORK" TO THE BASIC R-S FLIP-FLOP.

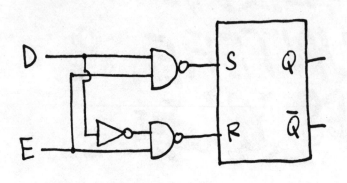

HERE "D" STANDS FOR *DATA*, AND "E" STANDS FOR *ENABLE*. NOTE THAT THE GATING NETWORK MAKES IT IMPOSSIBLE FOR R AND S TO BE ZERO SIMULTANEOUSLY.

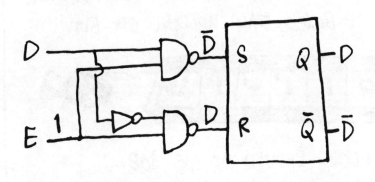

WHEN E=1, THEN R=D AND S=$\bar{D}$ (NOT-D). HENCE, THE VALUE OF D IS STORED AT Q. IN OTHER WORDS, E=1 **ENABLES** THE BIT D TO BE LOADED INTO THE FLIP-FLOP.

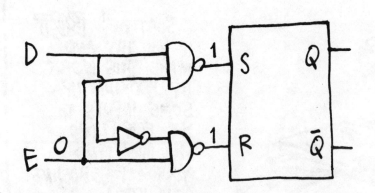

WHEN E=0, S AND R BOTH BECOME 1, AND THE FLIP-FLOP DOES NOT CHANGE. THAT IS, E=0 BLOCKS THE ARRIVAL OF MORE DATA.

COMPUTERS ARE
BLACK BOXES MADE
OF BLACK BOXES
MADE OF BLACK BOXES...

SO—IN THE SPIRIT OF
IGNORING THE INNER WORKINGS
ONCE THEY'RE UNDERSTOOD
[OR EVEN WITHOUT EVER
UNDERSTANDING THEM],
WE INCORPORATE THE
GATING NETWORK
INTO THE BOX, AND DRAW
THE GATED LATCH LIKE
SO

FRILLS

THEN HERE'S A **PARALLEL REGISTER**: NOT THE ONLY
KIND OF REGISTER, BUT A GENUINE MEMBER OF THE BREED!

DATA IN

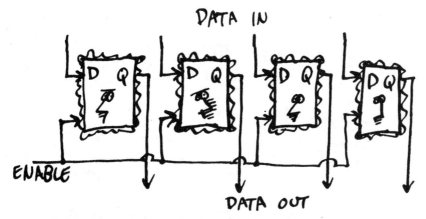

ON E=1,
FOUR BITS
ARE SIMUL-
TANEOUSLY
LOADED
INTO THE
LATCHES!

ENABLE

DATA OUT

NOW WHAT CONTROLS THE "ENABLE" INPUT?

A BASIC FACT OF COMPUTER LIFE:

AS SOON AS YOU BEGIN STORING DATA, QUESTIONS OF *TIMING* ARISE: HOW LONG DO YOU STORE IT? WHEN DO YOU MOVE IT? HOW DO YOU SYNCHRONIZE SIGNALS? THESE ISSUES ARE SO CRITICAL THAT LOGIC WITH MEMORY IS CALLED **SEQUENTIAL,** TO DISTINGUISH IT FROM THE PURELY **COMBINATIONAL** LOGIC OF MEMORY-LESS NETWORKS. TO KEEP THE SEQUENTIAL LOGIC IN STEP,

➡ ALL COMPUTERS HAVE CLOCKS!

THE CLOCK'S PULSE IS THE COMPUTER'S HEARTBEAT—ONLY INSTEAD OF A WARM, RAGGED HUMAN HEARTBEAT, LIKE THIS—

THE COMPUTER'S PULSE IS SQUARE AND COLD:

1

0

ONE PULSE → ONE CYCLE ←

ONE **CLOCK** PULSE IS THE BURST OF CURRENT WHEN CLOCK OUTPUT = 1. ONE **CYCLE** IS THE INTERVAL FROM THE BEGINNING OF A PULSE TO THE BEGINNING OF THE NEXT. DEPENDING ON THE COMPUTER, THE CLOCK FREQUENCY MAY BE HUNDREDS OF THOUSANDS TO *BILLIONS* OF CYCLES PER SECOND!

SLOW COMPUTER:

$\leftarrow \frac{1}{1000000}$ SEC $\longrightarrow$

FAST COMPUTER:

THE IDEA OF USING A CLOCK IS THAT THE COMPUTER'S LOGICAL STATE SHOULD CHANGE *ONLY* ON THE CLOCK PULSE. IDEALLY, WHEN THE CLOCK HITS 1, ALL SIGNALS MOVE, THEN STOP ON CLOCK = 0. THEN GO... THEN STOP... THEN GO...

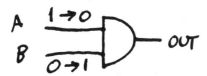

GO STOP GO STOP...

A TYPICAL EXAMPLE IS TO ATTACH THE CLOCK TO THE "ENABLE" INPUT OF A GATED LATCH, IN WHICH CASE THE LATCH BECOMES KNOWN AS A "D FLIP-FLOP."

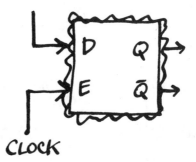

CLOCK

THEN A NEW BIT OF DATA IS LOADED AT EVERY CLOCK PULSE!

HEE HEE

UNFORTUNATELY, THINGS ARE RARELY IDEAL! IT TAKES A NON-ZERO TIME FOR A SIGNAL TO PASS ALONG A WIRE, SO THINGS ARE NEVER PERFECTLY SYNCHRONIZED. FOR EXAMPLE, SUPPOSE AT AN *AND* GATE, ONE INPUT IS CHANGING FROM 1 TO 0, AND THE OTHER FROM 0 TO 1:

A $1 \to 0$

B $0 \to 1$ — OUT

IF A CHANGES AFTER B, THE OUTPUT WILL HAVE AN UNWANTED PULSE:

CLOCK

A ← LATE!

B

OUT

THAT PULSE IS A *GLITCH*, AND BRIEF AS IT IS, IT CAN CAUSE A FLIP-FLOP TO FLOP!

WE'RE UNAVOIDABLE!

THE GLITCH IS DEFEATED BY THE
MASTER-SLAVE FLIP-FLOP:

WE WERE BORN EQUAL, MASTER, AND ONLY MY POSITION MAKES ME A SLAVE!

THE INVERTED CLOCK SIGNAL TO THE SLAVE FLIP-FLOP DELAYS THE DATA INPUT FROM ARRIVING AT THE SLAVE UNTIL THE **END** OF A CLOCK PULSE, AFTER ALL GLITCHES HAVE DIED OUT. FOR EXAMPLE, SUPPOSE WE WANT TO LOAD THE BIT **1** INTO THE FLIP-FLOP.

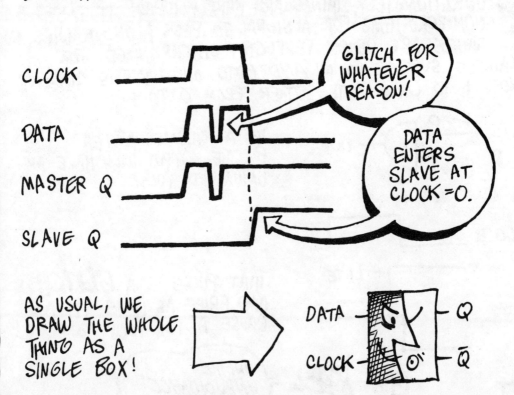

GLITCH, FOR WHATEVER REASON!

DATA ENTERS SLAVE AT CLOCK = 0.

AS USUAL, WE DRAW THE WHOLE THING AS A SINGLE BOX!

STRINGING A NUMBER OF MASTER-SLAVE FLIP-FLOPS TOGETHER MAKES A

SHIFT REGISTER:

DATA ENTER A SHIFT REGISTER ONE BIT AT A TIME, SHIFTING TO THE RIGHT WITH EACH NEW CLOCK PULSE.

FOR EXAMPLE, THE NIBBLE 1101 WOULD ENTER THE SHIFT REGISTER LIKE THIS:

EACH CLOCK PULSE BRINGS A NEW BIT INTO THE REGISTER. (WHY DOESN'T THE BIT TRAVEL ALL THE WAY THROUGH ON ONE PULSE? BECAUSE OF THE MASTER-SLAVE FLIP-FLOPS!)

LIKEWISE, THE NIBBLE SHIFTS **OUT** ONE BIT AT A TIME.

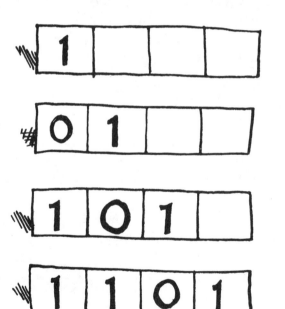

 SHIFT REGISTERS ARE USEFUL WHEN INFORMATION IS TO BE TRANSMITTED **SERIALLY**, OR ONE BIT AT A TIME.

FINALLY, A SPECIAL KIND OF REGISTER: THE **COUNTER.**

IS THAT LIKE THE COUNTER MONTE CRISTO?

A COUNTER IS JUST WHAT IT SOUNDS LIKE: SOMETHING THAT COUNTS. IN OTHER WORDS, IT'S A REGISTER THAT *INCREMENTS* ITSELF— ADDS 1 TO ITS CONTENTS— WHENEVER A "COUNT" SIGNAL ARRIVES:

COUNT IN

0	0	0	0	0	0	0	0

0	0	0	0	0	0	0	1

0	0	0	0	0	0	1	0

ETC!

DESCRIBED IN THAT WAY, A COUNTER SOUNDS EASY TO MAKE: JUST COMBINE AN ADDER WITH A REGISTER! THIS WOULD IN FACT WORK, BUT THERE'S AN EVEN SLICKER WAY, BASED ON ANOTHER FANCY FLIP-FLOP. CONSIDER THIS MASTER-SLAVE FLIP-FLOP, COUPLED BACK ON ITSELF:

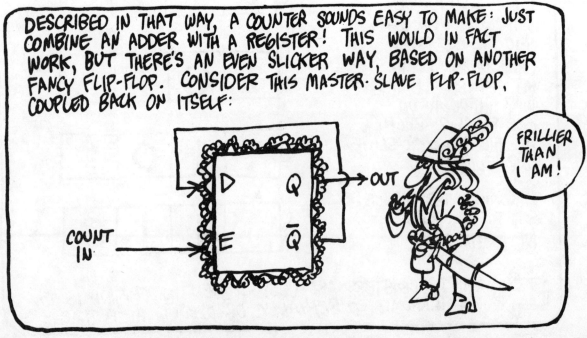

D   Q   → OUT

COUNT IN

E   Q̄

FRILLIER THAN I AM!

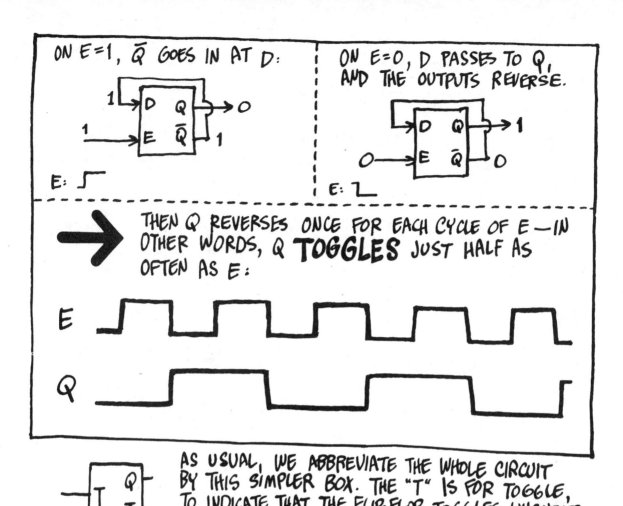

ON E=1, Q̄ GOES IN AT D:

ON E=0, D PASSES TO Q, AND THE OUTPUTS REVERSE.

E: ⌐

E: ⌐_

THEN Q REVERSES ONCE FOR EACH CYCLE OF E —IN OTHER WORDS, Q **TOGGLES** JUST HALF AS OFTEN AS E:

E

Q

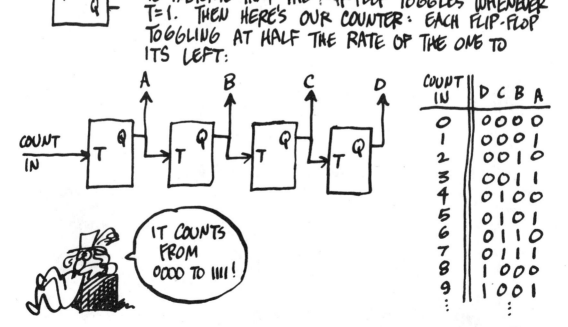

AS USUAL, WE ABBREVIATE THE WHOLE CIRCUIT BY THIS SIMPLER BOX. THE "T" IS FOR TOGGLE, TO INDICATE THAT THE FLIP-FLOP TOGGLES WHENEVER T=1. THEN HERE'S OUR COUNTER: EACH FLIP-FLOP TOGGLING AT HALF THE RATE OF THE ONE TO ITS LEFT:

IT COUNTS FROM 0000 TO 1111!

COUNT IN	D C B A
0	0 0 0 0
1	0 0 0 1
2	0 0 1 0
3	0 0 1 1
4	0 1 0 0
5	0 1 0 1
6	0 1 1 0
7	0 1 1 1
8	1 0 0 0
9	1 0 0 1
⋮	⋮

147

A FEW ITEMS OF NOTE:

1 THIS COUNTER IS CALLED AN "ASYNCHRONOUS RIPPLE COUNTER," BECAUSE THE COUNT RIPPLES THROUGH FROM ONE FLIP-FLOP TO THE NEXT. THIS CAUSES A SLIGHT DELAY BEFORE THE COUNT IS REGISTERED.

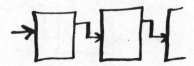

I LOVE RIPPLE

2 WHEN THE 16TH COUNT PULSE ARRIVES, THE COUNTER RETURNS TO 0. TO GO HIGHER THAN 15, MORE FLIP-FLOPS ARE NEEDED.

THIS 14-BIT COUNTER CAN GO FROM 0 TO $2^{14}-1 = 16,383$

3 THE NTH FLIP-FLOP IN A RIPPLE COUNTER **DIVIDES** THE INCOMING PULSE BY 2^n. THIS IS THE PRINCIPLE ON WHICH DIGITAL WATCHES ARE BASED: A HIGH-FREQUENCY INTERNAL CLOCK PULSE IS DIVIDED TO A RATE OF PRECISELY ONE CYCLE PER SECOND.

INTERNAL CLOCK:
OUTPUT:

|←—— 1 SECOND ——→|

4 THERE ARE ALSO **SYNCHRONOUS** COUNTERS, WHICH REGISTER ALL BITS SIMULTANEOUSLY, AND COUNTERS WHICH RETURN TO 0 ON ANY PREASSIGNED NUMBER. IN ANY CASE, FROM NOW ON, A COUNTER IS JUST ANOTHER BLACK BOX !!

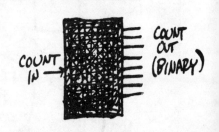

COUNT IN → COUNT OUT (BINARY)

EXERCISES

THE AMAZING *NAND*:

1. SHOW THAT

A ⎯▷○⎯ IS THE SAME AS ⎯▷○⎯

A, B ⎯▷○⎯▷○⎯ IS THE SAME AS ⎯▷⎯ (AND)

A ⎯▷○⎯, B ⎯▷○⎯ ⎯▷○⎯ IS THE SAME AS ⎯▷⎯ (OR)

CONCLUDE THAT ⟹ ALL LOGIC CAN BE DERIVED FROM THE SINGLE RELATION *NAND*!!!

2. CAN THE SAME BE DONE WITH *NOR*?

3. SHOW THAT

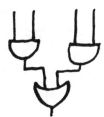

IS THE SAME AS

REDRAW THE ADDER ON P. 126 USING ONLY *NAND*-GATES.

4. GIVEN A 4-BIT SHIFT REGISTER,

SHOW ITS CONTENTS AFTER EACH OF FOUR CLOCK PULSES AS THE NIBBLE 0011 IS ENTERED.

5. HOW WOULD YOU ATTACH A BUZZER TO A COUNTER TO SOUND WHEN THE COUNT HITS NINE (=1001 IN BINARY)? HINT: LOOK AT THE SEAT BELT BUZZER ON P. 109.

6. CONVINCE YOURSELF THAT ATTACHING INVERTERS TO THE OUTPUTS MAKES A COUNTER COUNT BACKWARDS.

NOW IN CASE YOU'RE FEELING STRANGLED BY SPAGHETTI—

THE TANGLED DIAGRAMS ON THE PRECEDING PAGES WERE NEVER INTENDED TO TRACE THE COMPLETE WIRING DIAGRAM OF ANY COMPUTER. RATHER, THEY ARE MEANT TO DEMONSTRATE HOW THE COMPUTER'S ESSENTIAL FUNCTIONS— MATH, COMPARISON, DECODING, DATA SELECTION AND STORAGE— ALL DEPEND ON SIMPLE LOGIC.

NOW THAT YOU PRESUMABLY BELIEVE IN THE POWER OF LOGIC, NO MORE WIRING DIAGRAMS ARE NEEDED!

ONWARD, TO HIGHER LEVELS!

IN THE INFANCY OF ELECTRONIC COMPUTING, MEMORY WAS ALWAYS MORE EXPENSIVE THAN SHEER COMPUTING POWER. PLENTY OF PROCESSING COULD BE DONE WITH RELATIVELY FEW COMPONENTS, BUT EVERY INCREASE IN MEMORY SIMPLY MEANT **MORE** — MORE ACTUAL, PHYSICAL PLACES TO STORE THINGS!

RESULT: BIG PROCESSORS, SMALL MEMORIES!

SINCE THEN, RESEARCH INTO MEMORY TECHNOLOGY HAS BROUGHT DOWN THE COST CONSIDERABLY. FOR A FEW HUNDRED DOLLARS YOU CAN BUY A MICRO WITH OVER 64,000 BYTES OF MEMORY, COMPARED WITH **ENIAC**'S MEMORY OF ABOUT 100 NUMBERS* — AT A COST OF MILLIONS!!

AND A HUMAN'S BILLIONS OF NEURONS, COSTING—?

*ENIAC DID NOT COMPUTE IN BINARY.

152

THE SAME RESEARCH EFFORT, HOWEVER, HAS PRODUCED A BEWILDERING ARRAY OF MEMORY TYPES AND TECHNOLOGIES!!

CARD MEMORIES, TAPE MEMORIES, DRUM, DISK, BUBBLE, OPTICAL, CORE, CHARGE-COUPLED DEVICE, AND SEMICONDUCTOR MEMORIES; VOLATILE AND NON-VOLATILE, DYNAMIC AND STATIC, DESTRUCTIVE AND NON DESTRUCTIVE, READ-WRITE, READ-ONLY, PROGRAMMABLE READ-ONLY, ERASABLE PROGRAMMABLE READ-ONLY... :PANT: :PUFF:

HAVE I FORGOTTEN ANYTHING?

I DON'T REMEMBER..

WELL, ONE HAS TO BEGIN SOMEWHERE!!

153

AN IMPORTANT
DISTINCTION EXISTS
BETWEEN

ELECTRONIC

AND

ELECTRO-
MECHANICAL

MEMORY DEVICES.

ELECTRONIC MEMORIES, WITH
NO MOVING PARTS, ARE
AS FAST AS THE REST OF
THE COMPUTER.

ELECTROMECHANICAL MEMORIES
HAVE MOVING PARTS, LIKE
DISKS OR REELS OF TAPE.
THIS MAKES THEM SLOW—
HOW SLOW DEPENDING
ON THE TYPE OF MEMORY.

YOU FOUND THAT FILE YET?

ELECTRONIC MEMORIES' SPEED
MAKES THEM IDEAL FOR THE
COMPUTER'S MAIN, OR INTERNAL
MEMORY, WHILE ELECTRO-
MECHANICAL MEMORIES ARE
USED FOR AUXILIARY STORAGE
OUTSIDE THE MACHINE.

ELECTROMAGNETIC MEMORIES
COMPENSATE FOR THEIR SLOWNESS
WITH A GIGANTIC CAPACITY.
ONE HARD DISK CAN STORE
UP TO TEN MILLION BYTES,
COMPARED WITH A TYPICAL MICRO'S
MAIN MEMORY OF 65,536
($=2^{16}$) BYTES.

INTERNAL MEMORY CAN BE THOUGHT OF AS A SIMPLE GRID, WITH A CELL AT EACH INTERSECTION. DEPENDING ON THE COMPUTER, EACH CELL CAN HOLD ONE BYTE, TWO BYTES, OR MORE.

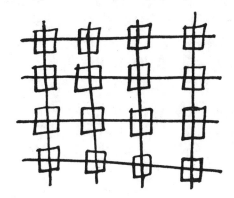

EVERY CELL HAS A UNIQUE **ADDRESS**, SPECIFYING WHERE IT SITS IN THE GRID.

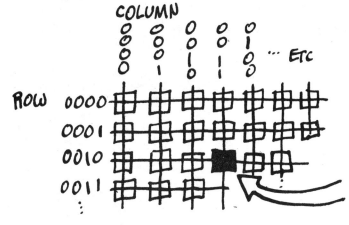

ADDRESS $\underbrace{0010}_{ROW}$ $\underbrace{0011}_{COLUMN}$

IN PRACTICE, THERE MAY BE MANY SUCH GRIDS, IN WHICH CASE THE ADDRESS SPECIFIES THE GRID NUMBER, AS WELL AS THE ROW AND COLUMN WITHIN IT.

ADDRESS $\underbrace{0101}_{GRID}$ $\underbrace{1001}_{ROW}$ $\underbrace{1110}_{COLUMN}$

NOTE: DO NOT CONFUSE A CELL'S ADDRESS WITH ITS CONTENTS!!

WHAT IS THE MAXIMUM NUMBER OF CELLS THE COMPUTER CAN ADDRESS? THIS DEPENDS ON THE LENGTH AND STRUCTURE OF THE COMPUTER'S "WORDS." FOR EXAMPLE, A 32-BIT MACHINE MAY INTERPRET THE FIRST 8 BITS AS AN INSTRUCTION...

8-BIT INSTRUCTION

`1 0 0 0 1 1 0 1 0 0 0 1 .... 0 1`

24-BIT ADDRESS

...AND THE REMAINING 24 BITS AS AN ADDRESS.

IN THAT CASE, ADDRESSES CAN BE ANYTHING BETWEEN

$$0 0 0 0 0 \cdots 0$$
AND
$$1 1 1 1 \cdots 1 = 2^{24} - 1$$

GIVING 2^{24} POSSIBLE MEMORY CELLS.

16,777,216, TO BE EXACT!

AN 8-BIT MICRO, ON THE OTHER HAND, MIGHT PROCESS THREE BYTES IN SUCCESSION:

`0 0 1 1 0 1 1 1`

AN INSTRUCTION,

`1 0 0 1 1 0 1 0`

THE FIRST HALF OF AN ADDRESS,

`0 0 0 1 0 1 0 0`

AND THE SECOND HALF OF AN ADDRESS

▶ HERE THE ADDRESS IS 16 BITS LONG, GIVING $2^{16} = 65,536$ POSSIBLE ADDRESSES.

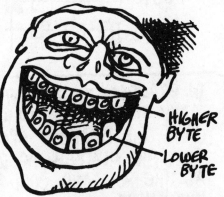

HIGHER BYTE
LOWER BYTE

16-BIT WORDS ARE OFTEN SPLIT LIKE THIS INTO HIGHER-LEVEL AND LOWER-LEVEL BYTES.

`1 0 0 0 1 1 0 1` `0 0 0 1 0 0 1 0`
HIGHER   LOWER

TO MAKE ADDRESSES SHORTER AND MORE READABLE, THEY'RE OFTEN EXPRESSED IN

HEXADECIMAL,

OR BASE-16, NUMERALS.

OUR FAVORITE!

$10_{HEX} = 16_{DECIMAL}$

$100_{HEX} = 16^2 = 256$

$1000_{HEX} = 16^3 = 4096$

⋮

ETC!

JUST AS BASE-10 NUMBERS REQUIRE THE DIGITS 0-9, SO HEXADECIMAL NEEDS DIGITS FROM 0 TO FIFTEEN. THE EXTRAS ARE REPRESENTED BY THE LETTERS A-F:

DECIMAL	0	1	2	3	4	5	6	7	8	9	10	11	12	13	14	15
HEX	0	1	2	3	4	5	6	7	8	9	A	B	C	D	E	F

FOR EXAMPLE:

$4A0D_{HEX} =$

4×16^3

$+ 10 \times 16^2$

$+ 0 \times 16$

$+ 13 \times 1$

―――――――

$18,957_{DECIMAL}$

TO CONVERT BINARY TO HEX: GROUP THE BINARY NUMBER INTO NIBBLES, STARTING FROM THE RIGHT. CONVERT EACH NIBBLE TO A HEX DIGIT!

101 1110 0101 1011

5　　C　　5　　B

TO CONVERT HEX TO BINARY, JUST REVERSE THE PROCESS.

FROM THE HARDWARE POINT OF VIEW, THERE ARE THREE
MAIN TYPES OF INTERNAL MEMORY.

CORE

MEMORIES USE
LITTLE MAGNETIC
DOUGHNUTS - "CORES."
EACH CORE CAN
BE ELECTRICALLY
MAGNETIZED IN ONE
OF TWO DIRECTIONS,
REPRESENTING
O AND 1.

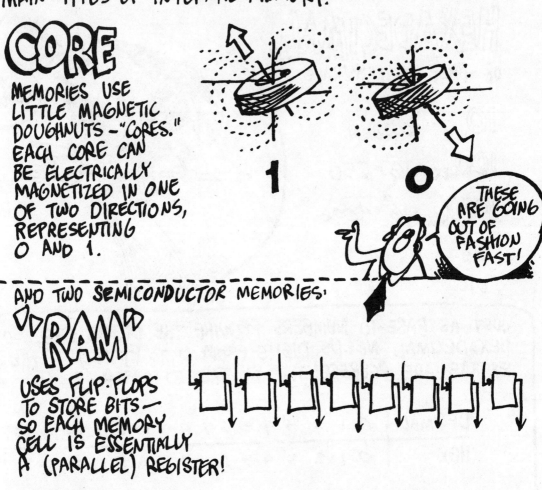

THESE ARE GOING OUT OF FASHION FAST!

AND TWO SEMICONDUCTOR MEMORIES:

RAM

USES FLIP-FLOPS
TO STORE BITS—
SO EACH MEMORY
CELL IS ESSENTIALLY
A (PARALLEL) REGISTER!

ROM

INDICATES A 1 OR
O AT EACH GRID
POINT BY THE
PRESENCE OR
ABSENCE OF AN
ELECTRIC CONNECTION
THERE.

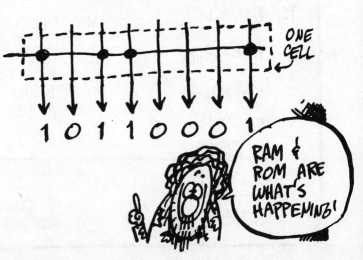

ONE CELL

1 0 1 1 0 0 0 1

RAM & ROM ARE WHAT'S HAPPENING!

RAM STANDS FOR "RANDOM ACCESS MEMORY," MEANING THAT ANY CELL CAN BE ACCESSED DIRECTLY. ROM AND CORE MEMORIES ALSO PROVIDE RANDOM ACCESS, BUT FOR SOME REASON RAM HOGGED THE NAME!

A CASE OF SPECIES CONFUSION...

ROM STANDS FOR "READ-ONLY MEMORY."

ROM-AN STYLE LETTERING

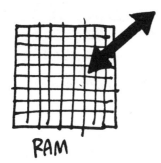

RAM

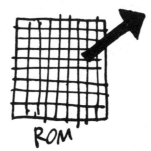

ROM

THE PRACTICAL DIFFERENCE BETWEEN THEM IS THAT YOU CAN ONLY READ WHAT'S IN ROM, WHILE WITH RAM YOU CAN READ THINGS OUT OR WRITE THEM IN WITH EQUAL EASE.

IN GENERAL!

WHEN YOU LOAD A PROGRAM INTO THE COMPUTER, IT IS STORED IN *RAM.*

UNFORTUNATELY, RAM IS *VOLATILE,*

SNORT!

 IT FORGETS EVERYTHING WHEN THE POWER IS TURNED OFF.

FOR EXAMPLE, I OWN A BATTERY-POWERED POCKET COMPUTER WITH 1680 BYTES OF RAM. IT CAN STORE UP TO TEN PROGRAMS *EVEN WHEN I TURN IT OFF,* BECAUSE IT KEEPS SOME ELECTRICITY RUNNING THROUGH MEMORY.

BUT WHEN THE BATTERY DIES... BYE BYE, PROGRAMS!

RAM VOLATILITY IS ONE REASON THAT THE MAGNIFICENT, INFALLIBLE COMPUTER IS VULNERABLE TO THE VAGARIES OF OUTMODED, ERRATIC POWER GENERATING STATIONS!

OOP!

ROM — "READ-ONLY MEMORY" —

ONCE ITS CONTENTS ARE ENTERED, CAN NEVER BE REWRITTEN.* ORDINARILY, ROM IS PROGRAMMED AT THE FACTORY, BUT THERE ARE NOW ALSO **PROMS** — PROGRAMMABLE ROMS — WHICH CAN BE CUSTOM-PROGRAMMED TO THE USER'S SPECIFICATIONS.

*EXCEPT FOR EPROM — ERASABLE PROGRAMMABLE ROM — BUT WE WON'T GET INTO THAT!

WHAT ARE YOU DOING ON PROM NIGHT?

GOING TO RADIO SHACK TO GET FIXED.

UNLIKE RAM, ROM IS **NON-VOLATILE:** IT KEEPS ITS CONTENTS EVEN WITHOUT POWER. AFTER ALL, IT'S NOTHING BUT A HUGE GRID OF WIRES WITH PHYSICAL CONNECTIONS AT SOME INTERSECTIONS. THE CONNECTIONS REMAIN, REGARDLESS OF ELECTRIC CURRENT.

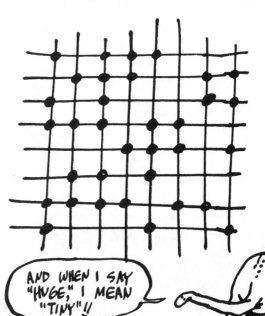

AND WHEN I SAY "HUGE," I MEAN "TINY"!!

SOME TYPICAL USES OF ROM:

MOST VIDEO
GAME CARTRIDGES
ARE
PROGRAMMED
IN ROM.
JUST PLUG
IT IN AND IT'S
READY TO GO!
BUT OF
COURSE, IT
CAN'T BE
REPROGRAMMED
EITHER...

YOU WANT TO PLAY ANOTHER GAME, YOU BUY ANOTHER GAME, SON..

A RATI COMPANY

MANY PERSONAL COMPUTERS HAVE THOUSANDS OF BYTES OF ROM TO STORE THE PROGRAM WHICH IN TURN ALLOWS THE MACHINE TO "UNDERSTAND" THE LANGUAGE CALLED BASIC.

IT'S CALLED "BUILT-IN BASIC!"

AND, AS WE'LL SEE, ROM PLAYS AN IMPORTANT ROLE IN THE COMPUTER'S CONTROL SECTION.

BEHIND THE EXPLOSIVE GROWTH OF RAM AND ROM IS...
THE INCREDIBLE SHRINKING TECHNOLOGY!

ETCHED ON SILICON CHIPS, THE DENSITY OF COMPONENTS PER CHIP HAS BEEN **DOUBLING** EVERY YEAR!

THE STANDARD MEASURE OF CHIP STORAGE IS THE **K**, SHORT FOR "KILO" ("CHILO" IS GREEK FOR 1000), IN COMPUTERESE IT MEANS 2^{10}, THE POWER OF TWO CLOSEST TO 1000:

ALMOST GREEK FOR ALMOST 1000!

$$K = 1024$$

THE FIRST RAM CHIP WITH 1K BITS OF STORAGE WAS A SENSATION — BUT NOW 64K IS COMMON, AND THE 256K CHIP HAS ARRIVED! WHAT'S NEXT?

KKK?

THE ANSWER?

mass storage.

AS THE NAME IMPLIES,
MASS STORAGE IS MEMORY
THAT CAN STORE A LOT!!
ALMOST ALL MASS STORAGE
DEVICES ARE *NON*-VOLATILE
AND HAVE A MECHANICAL
COMPONENT THAT MAKES THEM
MUCH SLOWER THAN ELECTRONIC
RANDOM ACCESS MEMORIES.

DISCUM VOBISCUM!

FOR EXAMPLE,

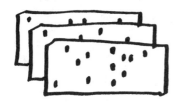

PUNCH CARDS.
THE CARDS OF JACQUARD, BABBAGE,
AND HOLLERITH ARE STILL IN USE!

PAPER TAPE
SAME IDEA AS PUNCH CARDS: A HOLE REPRESENTS
1, A NON-HOLE 0.

MAGNETIC TAPE
STORES BITS AS SMALL MAGNETIC REGIONS, WHICH MAY
BE MAGNETIZED IN ONE OF TWO DIRECTIONS,
REPRESENTING 1 OR 0.

FASTER, LESS BULKY, AND THE CURRENT STORAGE OF CHOICE IS THE

MAGNETIC DISK

DISKS ALSO STORE BITS AS TINY MAGNETIZED REGIONS — UP TO 10 MILLION BYTES PER DISK!

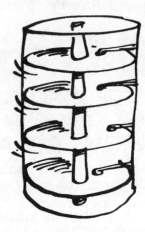

A BIG COMPUTER SYSTEM USUALLY HAS MULTIPLE DISK DRIVES, WITH PHONOGRAPH-ARMLIKE READ/WRITE HEADS DARTING BACK AND FORTH ACROSS THE WHIRLING PLATTERS.

FLOPPIES

ARE SMALL, LOW-COST MAGNETIC DISKS MADE OF PLASTIC. THEY ALWAYS STAY IN THEIR JACKETS, BECAUSE A SPECK OF DUST CAN CREATE A MONSTER GLITCH!

LOVE THAT DUST!

OTHER, MORE EXOTIC MASS STORAGE TECHNOLOGIES INCLUDE *BUBBLE* MEMORIES, *CHARGE-COUPLED DEVICES*, AND *OPTICAL DISKS* READ BY LASERS.

LIKE INTERNAL MEMORY, MASS STORAGE MUST BE ORGANIZED, OR "FORMATTED." TAKE THE FLOPPY DISK FOR EXAMPLE:

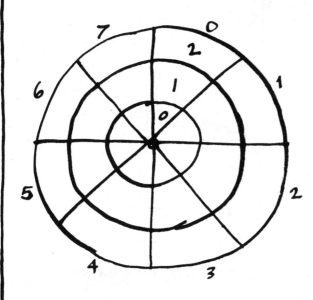

FLOPPIES ARE FORMATTED INTO RINGS AND SECTORS — THREE RINGS AND EIGHT SECTORS, IN THIS VERY OVER-SIMPLIFIED DISK. (IT'S MORE LIKE 26 SECTORS AND 77 RINGS IN A GENUINE DISK.)

TO ACCESS A PARTICULAR BLOCK OF DATA, YOU SPECIFY THE RING NUMBER AND SECTOR NUMBER. THEN THE DISK DRIVE

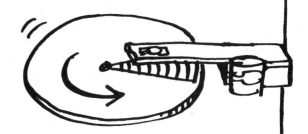

1) SPINS THE DISK UNTIL THAT SECTOR LIES UNDER THE READ/WRITE HEAD

2) MOVES THE HEAD IN OR OUT TO THE PROPER RING.

 THIS PROCESS TAKES MILLISECONDS — AN ETERNITY TO A COMPUTER!

SOME TYPICAL USES OF MASS STORAGE:

A GERBIL RANCHER, USING A MICROCOMPUTER TO IMPROVE PRODUCTIVITY, BUYS THE APPROPRIATE PROGRAMS (FROM GERBYTE, INC.) STORED ON FLOPPIES.

AND VERY TASTY THEY ARE, TOO!

THE ONLY PEOPLE WHO CAN SEE THIS LIST ARE PEOPLE WHO AREN'T ON THIS LIST...

AND EVERYBODY'S ON THIS LIST...

SO WHO AM I?

A GOVERNMENT AGENCY (TAKE YOUR PICK) MAINTAINS FILES ON THE CITIZENRY, STORED ON HARD DISK...

THE PHONE COMPANY STORES IN BUBBLE MEMORY THE MESSAGE: "THE NUMBER YOU HAVE REACHED IS NOT IN SERVICE..."

HM... SOUNDS LIKE A VERBAL GERBIL...

WELL, YOU GET THE PICTURE... NOW IT'S TIME TO MOVE ON...

GETTING EVERYTHING UNDER CONTROL

IN WHICH ALL THE BLACK BOXES ARE FINALLY SEEN TO FIT TOGETHER...

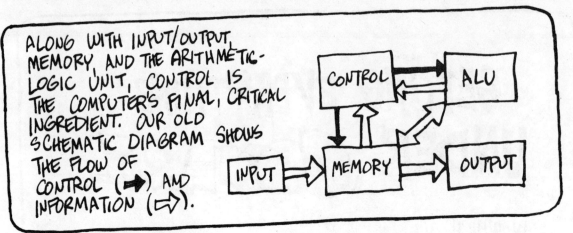

ALONG WITH INPUT/OUTPUT, MEMORY, AND THE ARITHMETIC-LOGIC UNIT, CONTROL IS THE COMPUTER'S FINAL, CRITICAL INGREDIENT. OUR OLD SCHEMATIC DIAGRAM SHOWS THE FLOW OF CONTROL (➡) AND INFORMATION (⇨).

IT HELPS TO REDRAW THIS DIAGRAM IN A WAY THAT BETTER REFLECTS A GENUINE COMPUTER DESIGN KNOWN AS "BUS ARCHITECTURE."

THE VERTICAL ARROWS, REPRESENTING ELECTRICAL PATHWAYS A BYTE OR MORE WIDE, ARE THE **BUSES.**

ACCORDING TO SIGNALS PASSED ALONG THE CONTROL BUS, ADDRESSES AND DATA GET ON AND OFF THE DATA/ADDRESS BUS, WITH THE PROVISO THAT ONLY ONE "PASSENGER" CAN RIDE THE BUS AT A TIME.

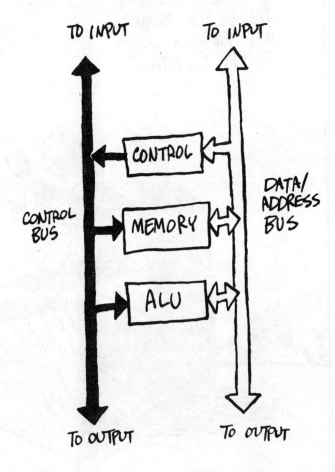

 NOTE THAT ALL THE ARROWS ON THE CONTROL BUS POINT **AWAY** FROM THE CONTROL SECTION.

171

LIKE ANYONE ELSE, CONTROL REVEALS ITS CHARACTER
BY ITS BEHAVIOR... SO LET'S FOLLOW WHAT HAPPENS
IN THIS OVERSIMPLIFIED COMPUTER, WHICH FLESHES
OUT THE DIAGRAM OF TWO PAGES BACK WITH SOME
ESSENTIAL COUNTERS AND REGISTERS.

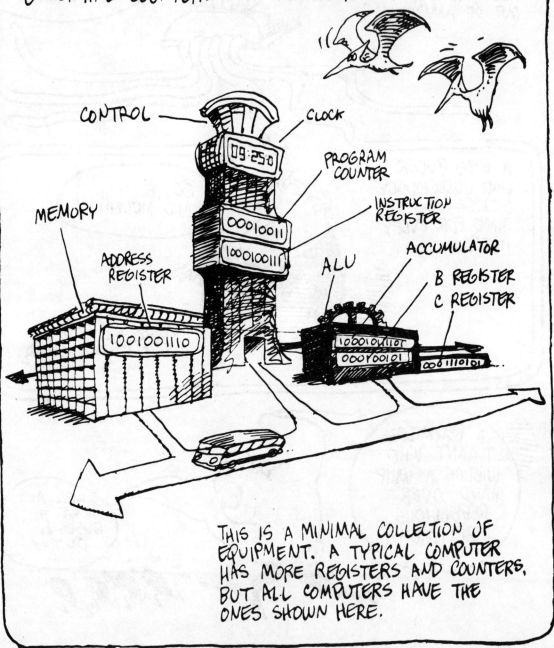

THIS IS A MINIMAL COLLECTION OF
EQUIPMENT. A TYPICAL COMPUTER
HAS MORE REGISTERS AND COUNTERS,
BUT ALL COMPUTERS HAVE THE
ONES SHOWN HERE.

HERE'S WHAT THEY'RE FOR:

PROGRAM COUNTER: TICKS OFF THE INSTRUCTIONS ONE BY ONE.

Two... Two...?

INSTRUCTION REGISTER: HOLDS AN ENCODED VERSION OF THE INSTRUCTION BEING PERFORMED.

"BOIL SPAGHETTI TEN MINUTES."

ADDRESS REGISTER: HOLDS THE ADDRESS OF WHATEVER IS TO ENTER OR LEAVE MEMORY.

GET ME BYTE #0101!

ACCUMULATOR: THE ALU'S MAIN REGISTER, KEEPING A RUNNING TOTAL OF ALU OPERATIONS.

COULDN'T SOLVE 1+1 WITHOUT IT!

B REGISTER: AN AUXILIARY REGISTER TO HOLD NUMBERS ON THEIR WAY TO ALU.

LIKE A MOTEL THAT RENTS ROOMS BY THE MICROSECOND!

C REGISTER: HOLDS DATA ON THE WAY TO OUTPUT.

IS THERE CONTROL IN THE OUTSIDE WORLD?

 IN FACT, CONTROL SPENDS MOST OF ITS TIME JUST MOVING THE CONTENTS OF THESE REGISTERS AROUND!

TO SEE HOW CONTROL WORKS, LET'S FOLLOW WHAT HAPPENS WHEN THE COMPUTER **ADDS TWO NUMBERS —** OUR VERY FIRST PROGRAM!

LIKE EVERYTHING ABOUT COMPUTERS, PROGRAMS CAN BE DESCRIBED AT VARIOUS LEVELS. WE BEGIN WITH

ASSEMBLY LANGUAGE,

WHICH SPECIFIES THE COMPUTER'S ACTUAL MOVES, BUT OMITS THE FINE DETAILS. AT THIS LEVEL, HERE'S HOW TO ADD TWO NUMBERS:

0. LOAD THE FIRST NUMBER INTO THE ACCUMULATOR.

1. ADD THE SECOND NUMBER (HOLDING THE SUM IN THE ACCUMULATOR).

2. OUTPUT THE CONTENTS OF THE ACCUMULATOR.

3. HALT.

CAN'T OMIT THAT!!

TO EXPRESS THIS IN PROPER ASSEMBLY LANGUAGE, WE MUST SPECIFY THE PRECISE LOCATION IN MEMORY OF THE TWO NUMBERS TO BE ADDED, AND CONDENSE THE WORDY STATEMENTS INTO MNEMONIC* ABBREVIATIONS. SUPPOSE, FOR EXAMPLE, THAT THE NUMBERS ARE STORED AT ADDRESSES 1E AND 1F (HEXADECIMAL). OUR PROGRAM BECOMES:

A TRUE ASSEMBLY-LANGUAGE PROGRAM!

0. LDA 1E   ("LOAD ACCUMULATOR WITH CONTENTS OF 1E")

1. ADD 1F   ("ADD CONTENTS OF 1F")

2. OUT   ("OUTPUT CONTENTS OF ACCUMULATOR.")

3. HALT

*MNEMONIC = MEMORY-AIDING

IN GENERAL, ASSEMBLY-LANGUAGE STATEMENTS HAVE TWO PARTS:

THE **OPERATOR**, WHICH DESCRIBES THE STEP TO BE PERFORMED

THE **OPERAND**, WHICH GIVES THE ADDRESS ON WHICH THE OPERATOR ACTS

AS IN: PERFORM AN APPENDECTOMY ON THE RESIDENT OF 151 FIRST STREET!

LDA 1E

NOTE HOWEVER! SOME OPERATORS DON'T NEED AN EXPLICIT OPERAND. "OUT", FOR INSTANCE, IS UNDERSTOOD TO APPLY TO THE ACCUMULATOR.

NOW THAT WE HAVE AN ASSEMBLY-LANGUAGE PROGRAM, HOW DO WE FEED IT TO THE MACHINE — WHICH ONLY UNDERSTANDS 0'S AND 1'S?

THE ANSWER IS CLEAR: WITHIN THE MACHINE, EACH **OPERATOR** IS **ENCODED** AS A STRING OF BITS CALLED ITS "OP-CODE." SOME SIMPLE SAMPLES:

TO ME, "001" MEANS "LDA!"

OPERATOR	OP-CODE
LDA	001
ADD	010
OUT	110
HALT	111

I STILL WANT TO KNOW WHAT "MEAN" MEANS!

THEN A MACHINE INSTRUCTION CONSISTS OF AN OP-CODE SEGMENT, OR "FIELD," FOLLOWED BY AN ADDRESS FIELD GIVING THE OPERAND IN BINARY:

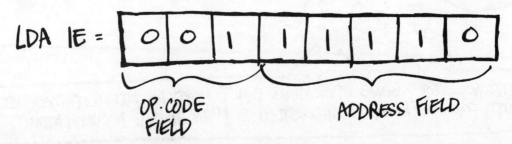

LDA 1E = | 0 | 0 | 1 | 1 | 1 | 1 | 1 | 0 |

OP-CODE FIELD   ADDRESS FIELD

176

SO HERE'S OUR PROGRAM TRANSLATED INTO MACHINE LANGUAGE:

0.	LDA 1E	001 11110
1.	ADD 1F	010 11111
2.	OUT	110 XXXXX
3.	HALT	111 XXXXX

ANY 5 BITS ARE O.K. FOR THESE ADDRESS FIELDS, AS THEY'LL BE IGNORED!

NOW,

(ASSUMING AN INPUT DEVICE)

THE PROGRAM STEPS ARE READ INTO CONSECUTIVE MEMORY ADDRESSES, BEGINNING WITH 0. THE CONTENTS OF MEMORY ARE THEN

ADDRESS	CONTENTS
0	001 11110
1	010 11111
2	110 00000
3	111 00000

NOTE THAT THE PROGRAM STEP NUMBER IS THE ADDRESS WHERE IT'S STORED!

AND WE ALSO NEED TO ENTER THE **DATA**: THE TWO NUMBERS TO BE ADDED. ANY TWO NUMBERS WILL DO, SAY 5 AND 121. THEY GO IN ADDRESSES 1E AND 1F:

1E	00000101
1F	01111001

HOW CAN THE COMPUTER DISTINGUISH DATA FROM INSTRUCTIONS? BY ASSUMING EVERYTHING IS AN INSTRUCTION, UNLESS INSTRUCTED TO DO OTHERWISE!!

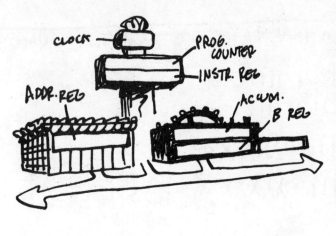

CLOCK

PROG. COUNTER

INSTR. REG

ADDR. REG

ACCUM.

B REG

ONCE THE PROGRAM IS STORED, CONTROL CAN BEGIN EXECUTION, IN A SERIES OF EVEN MORE PRIMITIVE STEPS CALLED **MICROINSTRUCTIONS**, ONE MICROINSTRUCTION OCCURRING WITH EACH CLOCK PULSE. ARE YOU READY FOR THE GORY DETAILS?

CONTROL BEGINS BY *FETCHING* THE FIRST INSTRUCTION. IT—

0.0. MOVES CONTENTS OF PROGRAM COUNTER (00000000 TO BEGIN WITH) TO ADDRESS REGISTER

0.1 MOVES CONTENTS OF THAT MEMORY ADDRESS TO INSTRUCTION REGISTER

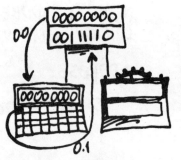

THE INSTRUCTION REGISTER NOW HOLDS THE FIRST INSTRUCTION. CONTROL "READS" IT AND—

0.2. MOVES THE INSTRUCTION REGISTER'S ADDRESS FIELD TO ADDRESS REGISTER

0.3. MOVES CONTENTS OF THAT MEMORY ADDRESS TO ACCUMULATOR

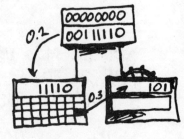

THE ACCUMULATOR IS NOW LOADED WITH THE FIRST PIECE OF DATA. ONE MICROINSTRUCTION REMAINS:

0.4 INCREMENT PROGRAM COUNTER

AND THAT'S STEP 0!

A BIT CONFUSED ? LET'S GO THROUGH IT AGAIN WITH THE NEXT STEP, **ADD**.

AGAIN CONTROL BEGINS WITH A "FETCH PHASE":

1.0 MOVE CONTENTS OF PROGRAM COUNTER (NOW 00000001)   TO   ADDRESS REGISTER

1.1 MOVE CONTENTS OF THAT ADDRESS   TO   INSTRUCTION REGISTER

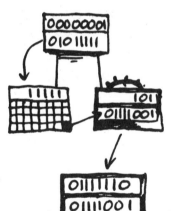

THE INSTRUCTION IN THE INSTRUCTION REGISTER, 010 11111, CAUSES CONTROL TO:

1.2 MOVE ADDRESS FIELD FROM INSTRUCTION REGISTER   TO   ADDRESS REGISTER

1.3 MOVE CONTENTS OF THAT MEMORY ADDRESS   TO   B REGISTER

1.4 SIGNAL THE ALU TO **ADD** AND PUT THE SUM   IN   ACCUMULATOR

AGAIN, THERE'S ONE MORE STEP:

1.5 INCREMENT PROGRAM COUNTER

GOOD NEWS !! IT GETS NO WORSE!

AND FINALLY?

WELL, LUCKILY THE LAST TWO INSTRUCTIONS ARE EASIER:

2.0 AND 2.1 ARE THE SAME FETCH INSTRUCTIONS AS BEFORE, PUTTING INSTRUCTION 2 ("OUT") IN THE INSTRUCTION REGISTER:

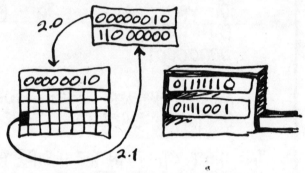

THIS OP-CODE (110) CAUSES CONTROL TO —

2.2. MOVE CONTENTS OF ACCUMULATOR TO C REGISTER

2.3. INCREMENT PROGRAM COUNTER

FINALLY, CONTROL FETCHES THE INSTRUCTION 111 ("HALT"), WHICH CAUSES CONTROL TO —

3.2 DO NOTHING

ARE YOU BEGINNING TO SEE WHAT KIND OF BEAST CONTROL REALLY IS ??

:SIGH:
I GUESS IT HAS TO COME OUT... SOB!!

WITHOUT TOO MANY DETAILS, YOU CAN THINK OF CONTROL ROUGHLY LIKE THIS:

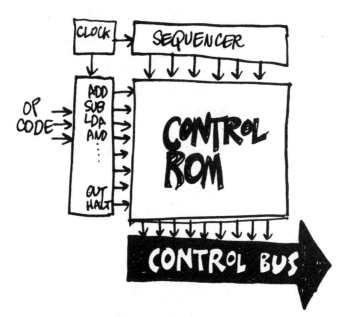

ITS INPUT CONSISTS OF CLOCK PULSES AND OP-CODES. ITS OUTPUT CONSISTS OF A **SEQUENCE** OF SIGNALS TO THE REGISTERS, COUNTERS, ALU, AND MEMORY.

THE "MICROPROGRAM," WHICH CONNECTS THE INPUTS TO THE PROPER OUTPUT COMBINATIONS, IS STORED IN A READ-ONLY MEMORY DEDICATED STRICTLY TO THIS PURPOSE.

THE FIRST COUPLE OF CLOCK PULSES CAUSE CONTROL TO FETCH AN INSTRUCTION...

IN REAL LIFE THE SITUATION IS MORE COMPLICATED IN
DETAIL BUT THE SAME IN PRINCIPLE. THERE ARE MORE
REGISTERS, AND OP-CODES ARE LONGER THAN THREE BITS,
ALLOWING CONTROL TO RESPOND TO A MUCH LARGER
SET OF INSTRUCTIONS. HERE'S THE INSTRUCTION SET
OF A GENUINE PROCESSOR, THE MOTOROLA 6800.

ARITHMETIC
- ADD
- ADD WITH CARRY
- SUBTRACT
- SUBTRACT WITH CARRY
- INCREMENT
- DECREMENT
- COMPARE
- NEGATE

LOGICAL
- AND
- OR
- EXCLUSIVE OR
- NOT
- SHIFT RIGHT
- SHIFT LEFT
- SHIFT RIGHT ARITHMETIC
- ROTATE RIGHT
- ROTATE LEFT
- TEST

DATA TRANSFER
- LOAD
- STORE
- MOVE
- CLEAR
- CLEAR CARRY
- CLEAR OVERFLOW
- SET CARRY
- SET OVERFLOW

BRANCH
- BRANCH
- BRANCH IF ZERO
- BRANCH IF NOT ZERO
- BRANCH IF EQUAL
- BRANCH IF NOT EQUAL
- BRANCH IF CARRY
- BRANCH IF NO CARRY
- BRANCH IF POSITIVE
- BRANCH IF NEGATIVE
- BRANCH IF OVERFLOW
- BRANCH IF NO OVERFLOW
- BRANCH IF GREATER THAN
- BRANCH IF GREATER THAN OR EQUAL
- BRANCH IF LESS THAN
- BRANCH IF LESS THAN OR EQUAL
- BRANCH IF HIGHER
- BRANCH IF NOT HIGHER
- BRANCH IF LOWER
- BRANCH IF NOT LOWER

SUBROUTINE CALL
- CALL SUBROUTINE

SUBROUTINE RETURN
- RETURN FROM SUBROUTINE
- RETURN FROM INTERRUPT

MISCELLANEOUS
- NO OPERATION
- PUSH
- POP
- WAIT
- ADJUST DECIMAL
- ENABLE INTERRUPT
- DISABLE INTERRUPT
- BREAK

ONE GROUP OF THESE INSTRUCTIONS DESERVES SPECIAL MENTION: THE *BRANCH*, OR *JUMP*, INSTRUCTIONS.

AS WE'LL SEE, THESE GIVE THE COMPUTER A LOT OF ITS "INTELLIGENCE." THEIR EFFECT IS TO **TRANSFER CONTROL** TO ANOTHER PART OF THE PROGRAM. THE SIMPLEST JUMP INSTRUCTION IS JUST PLAIN "JUMP," AS IN:

JMP 123

⟹ "JMP 123" CAUSES CONTROL TO ENTER 123 IN THE PROGRAM COUNTER... AND PROCEED WITH THE PROGRAM FROM THERE.

EVEN "SMARTER" ARE CONDITIONAL JUMPS. THEY TRANSFER CONTROL **IF** SOME CONDITION IS SATISFIED: FOR INSTANCE, "JUMP IF ZERO" MEANS JUMP IF THE ACCUMULATOR HOLDS 0.

JZ 321

OTHERWISE, DON'T JUMP!

11001001

SO YOU SEE, CONTROL IS NO TYRANT AT ALL. IT ONLY DOES WHAT IT'S TOLD— COMPLETELY AUTOMATICALLY!!

IF YOU REALLY WANT TO IMAGINE THE CONTROL SECTION'S PERSONALITY, THINK OF A PERFECTLY EFFICIENT *BUREAUCRAT*, ACTING IN STRICT OBEDIENCE TO THE COMPUTER'S 'REAL BOSS': THE **PROGRAM!**

184

IF PROGRAMS REALLY RULE THE COMPUTER, THEY DESERVE A PROPER SCIENTIFIC NAME... SOMETHING IN GREEK OR LATIN, PREFERABLY...

TECHNICALCULUS?
REGULA RATIONOCEROUS?
CEPHALONEURALGIA?

* *

BUT THAT'S NOT HOW IT IS IN COMPUTER SCIENCE... INSTEAD, PROGRAMS IN GENERAL ARE CALLED SOFTWARE, TO DISTINGUISH THEM FROM THE CIRCUIT BOARDS, CATHODE RAY MONITORS, DISK DRIVES, KEYBOARDS, AND OTHER ITEMS OF COMPUTER HARDWARE.

HARDWARE

SOFTWARE

TUPPERWARE

WHAT'S REALLY FUNNY ABOUT THE NAME IS THAT SOFTWARE IS ONE OF THE *HARDEST* THINGS ABOUT COMPUTING!

IT SOFTENS THE BRAIN!

WHILE HARDWARE HAS BEEN DROPPING IN PRICE AND GROWING IN POWER, SOFTWARE ONLY GETS MORE HORRENDOUSLY COMPLEX!

GET ME A HAND TRUCK!

WE SEE SMALLER AND SMALLER CHIPS WITH BIGGER & BIGGER MANUALS!

IT'S OFTEN IMPOSSIBLE TO ESTIMATE HOW MUCH TIME, MONEY, AND AGONY A GIVEN SOFTWARE PROBLEM WILL COST TO SOLVE... WHAT A WAY TO RUN A BUSINESS!

THE THRILL OF COMPUTING!

LIKEWISE THERE'S A DIFFERENCE BETWEEN THE IMAGE OF HARDWARE AND SOFTWARE WORKERS —

HARDWARE TYPES ARE ENGINEERS... INTO GADGETS... MOSTLY MEN... BOUND BY THE LAWS OF PHYSICS...

PROGRAMMERS HAVE NO TOOL BUT THEIR BRAINS... THEY'RE MORE OFTEN WOMEN... SUPPOSED TO BE SOLITARY DREAMERS WHOSE IDEAS HAVE NOTHING TO DO WITH THE LAWS OF PHYSICS!!

GRONK!

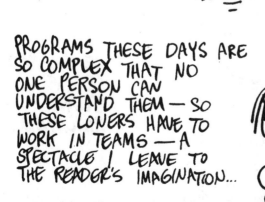

PROGRAMS THESE DAYS ARE SO COMPLEX THAT NO ONE PERSON CAN UNDERSTAND THEM — SO THESE LONERS HAVE TO WORK IN TEAMS — A SPECTACLE I LEAVE TO THE READER'S IMAGINATION...

WHILE ADA LOVELACE WAS THE ORIGINAL PROGRAMMER, THE FIRST PERSON TO PROVE THE FULL POWER OF SOFTWARE WAS **ALAN TURING** (1912-1954)

TURING, WHO ENJOYED LONG-DISTANCE RUNNING BACK WHEN THAT WAS CONSIDERED WEIRD, PROBABLY WENT INTO COMPUTERS TO SHRINK THE SIZE OF HIS JOGGING CLOCK.

IT'S MAKING MY STRIDE LOPSIDED!

IN 1936 HE DREAMED UP THE *TURING MACHINE*...

BONG! BONG!

TURING MACHINES AREN'T REAL MACHINES... THEY'RE ABSTRACT MACHINES, EXISTING ONLY IN THEORY...

A SOFTWARE ENGINEER'S DREAM — NO HARDWARE!

ROUGHLY SPEAKING, A TURING MACHINE IS AN INPUT-OUTPUT DEVICE: A BLACK BOX THAT READS A SEQUENCE OF O's AND 1's.

THE OUTPUT DEPENDS ONLY ON THE PRESENT INPUT (O OR 1) AND THE PREVIOUS OUTPUT.

THE NATURE OF THE OUTPUT IS UNIMPORTANT.

THE MAIN THING IS THAT THE CHANGES FROM ONE OUTPUT STATE TO THE NEXT ARE GIVEN BY DEFINITE RULES, CALLED THE *TRANSITION RULES*.

THE REASON TURING MACHINES ARE IMPORTANT IS THAT THEY ARE A A WAY OF THINKING PHYSICALLY ABOUT LOGIC. ANY WELL-DEFINED, STEP-BY-STEP LOGICAL PROCEDURE CAN BE EMBODIED IN SOME TURING MACHINE.

TOOT

THERE'S A TURING MACHINE THAT CAN ADD!

*FOR DETAILS, SEE J. WEIZENBAUM'S COMPUTER POWER AND HUMAN REASON, CHAPTER 2.

WHAT TURING PROVED: IT'S THEORETICALLY POSSIBLE TO CONSTRUCT A SINGLE TURING MACHINE, THE

UNIVERSAL TURING MACHINE,

WHICH CAN IMITATE ALL OTHER TURING MACHINES!!!

FOR A SMALL THEORETICAL DOWN PAYMENT!

WOW!

THE TRICK IS THAT THE UNIVERSAL TURING MACHINE CAN...

read instructions!

THAT IS, TO MAKE THE UNIVERSAL TURING MACHINE (**U**) ACT LIKE MACHINE **T**, YOU ENCODE **T**'S TRANSITION RULES ONTO **U**'S TAPE. AT EACH STEP, **U** OBSERVES ITS OWN INPUT, THEN REFERS TO **T**'S TRANSITION RULES TO SEE WHAT TO DO.

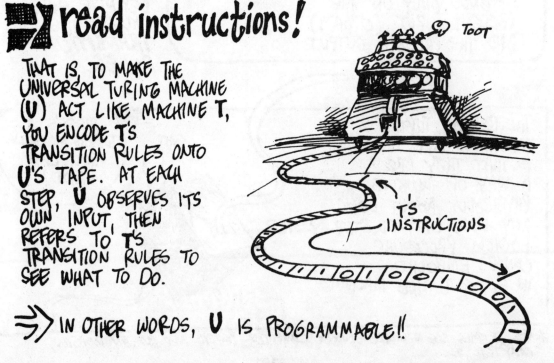

TOOT

T'S INSTRUCTIONS

⇒ IN OTHER WORDS, **U** IS PROGRAMMABLE!!

THE IMPLICATIONS
ARE STAGGERING:
A SINGLE,
PROGRAMMABLE
MACHINE CAN
PERFORM **ANY**
WELL·DEFINED,
STEP·BY·STEP
LOGICAL PROCEDURE.
(REMEMBER, TURING
SAW THIS TEN YEARS
BEFORE A REAL
COMPUTER WAS BUILT.)

STAGGERING
IMPLICATION

JOHN VON NEUMANN CARRIED TURING'S IDEAS A STEP
FURTHER. VON NEUMANN REALIZED THAT ONE COULD:

**BUILD A
MACHINE X
WHICH BUILDS
OTHER MACHINES
FROM PLANS
ENCODED ON
TAPE...**

**FEED X THE
PLANS TO
ITSELF!**

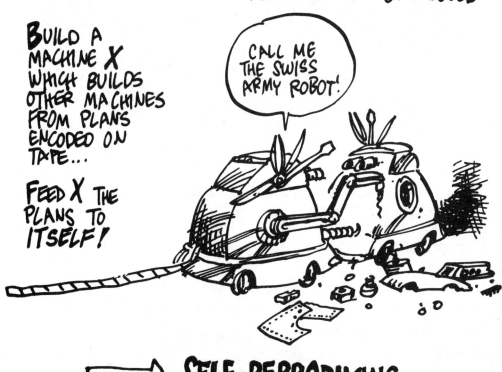

CALL ME
THE SWISS
ARMY ROBOT!

**SELF-REPRODUCING
MACHINES** ARE POSSIBLE!!

THE DIGITAL COMPUTER IS A FANCY UNIVERSAL TURING MACHINE COME TO LIFE.

IF YOU CALL THAT "LIFE..."

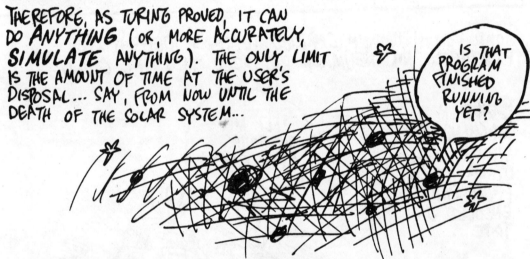

THEREFORE, AS TURING PROVED, IT CAN DO *ANYTHING* (OR, MORE ACCURATELY, *SIMULATE* ANYTHING). THE ONLY LIMIT IS THE AMOUNT OF TIME AT THE USER'S DISPOSAL... SAY, FROM NOW UNTIL THE DEATH OF THE SOLAR SYSTEM...

IS THAT PROGRAM FINISHED RUNNING YET?

TO BE PERFECTLY HONEST, THERE ARE A COUPLE OF OTHER QUALIFICATIONS ON THAT "ANYTHING." WHAT KIND OF "ANYTHING" CAN A COMPUTER DO?

CAN IT THINK?

CAN IT THWIM?

IN A WORD, COMPUTERS DO

ALGORITHMS

FROM AL-KHWARISMI, REMEMBER?

AN ALGORITHM IS SIMPLY ANY WELL DEFINED, STEP-BY-STEP PROCEDURE: A RECIPE, IF YOU WILL!

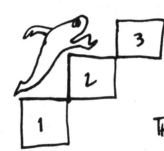

STEP-BY-STEP, MEANING EACH STEP IS COMPLETED BEFORE THE NEXT IS BEGUN.

WELL DEFINED, MEANING EACH STEP IS COMPLETELY DETERMINED BY CURRENT INPUT AND THE RESULTS OF PREVIOUS STEPS. NO AMBIGUITY ALLOWED!

EXAMPLES OF ALGORITHMS:

"IF NUCLEAR WARHEADS ARE FALLING LIKE HAILSTONES, I WILL LIE DOWN AND TRY TO ENJOY IT.

OTHERWISE, I WILL GO TO WORK AS USUAL."

IT'S AN ALGORITHM BECAUSE I ALWAYS KNOW WHAT TO DO:

1. CHECK TO SEE IF WARHEADS ARE FALLING
2. IF YES, LIE DOWN + ENJOY!
3. IF NO, GO TO WORK.

IT'S REASSURING TO HAVE THESE THINGS SPELLED OUT!

LIKEWISE, ALGEBRAIC FORMULAS REPRESENT ALGORITHMS

$y = x^2 + 2x + 10$ MEANS —

(1) INPUT A NUMBER x
(2) MULTIPLY x TIMES ITSELF
(3) MULTIPLY x TIMES 2
(4) ADD THE RESULTS OF (2) AND (3)
(5) ADD 10 TO THE RESULT OF (4)

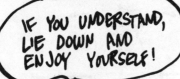

IF YOU UNDERSTAND, LIE DOWN AND ENJOY YOURSELF!

EXAMPLES OF **NON**-ALGORITHMS:

"IF NUCLEAR WARHEADS ARE FALLING LIKE HAILSTONES, LIE DOWN AND TRY TO ENJOY IT."

AND IN THE MEANTIME?

THIS FAILS TO TELL YOU WHAT TO DO IF NO WARHEADS ARE FALLING... SO IT'S NOT WELL DEFINED.

ANOTHER?

HOW ABOUT

$$y = x^2 + + 2x - 10 ?$$

MOST IMPROPER!

THIS IS NO ALGORITHM BECAUSE IT'S NOT EXPRESSED IN PROPER "ALGEBRAIC GRAMMAR." WE ASSIGN NO MEANING TO THE SYMBOLS "++".

IF YOU TRY TO MAKE A COMPUTER DO A NON-ALGORITHM, IT WILL JUST SIT THERE FLASHING ERROR MESSAGES!

SOME STANDARD SYMBOLS ARE USED TO MAKE ALGORITHMS EASIER TO FOLLOW. EACH STEP IS REPRESENTED BY A SPECIALLY SHAPED — WHAT ELSE? — BOX. THE SHAPE INDICATES WHAT TYPE OF STEP IS TO BE EXECUTED:

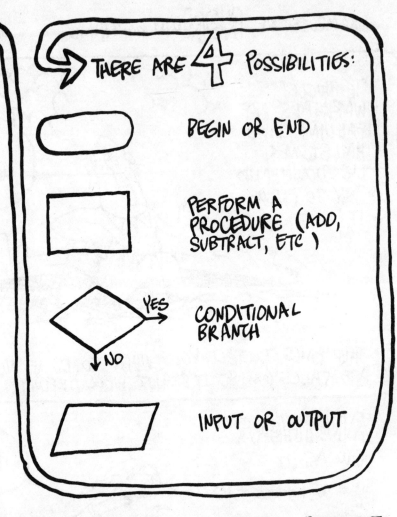

THERE ARE 4 POSSIBILITIES:

BEGIN OR END

PERFORM A PROCEDURE (ADD, SUBTRACT, ETC.)

YES

NO

CONDITIONAL BRANCH

INPUT OR OUTPUT

THE "FLOW" OF THE ALGORITHM IS REPRESENTED BY ARROWS →, AND WHEN ALL THE SYMBOLS ARE COMBINED, IT'S A

FLOW CHART

GO WITH THE FLOW...

HERE ARE THE
FLOW CHARTS
OF THE
ALGORITHMS
FROM A
COUPLE OF PAGES
BACK:

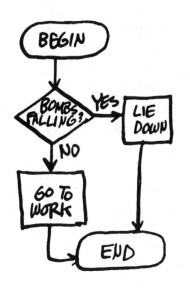

IN BOTH ALGORITHMS, THE FLOW PROCEEDS
IN ONE DIRECTION, FROM START TO FINISH.

- -

IT'S ALSO POSSIBLE FOR THE FLOW OF
ALGORITHMS TO JUMP FORWARD
OR BACKWARD. FOR EXAMPLE,
LET'S REWRITE THAT FIRST
ALGORITHM:

1. IF BOMBS ARE FALLING,
   GO TO STEP 2. OTHERWISE,
   GO TO STEP 4.

2. LIE DOWN AND ENJOY!

3. GO TO STEP 6.

4. LEAD A NORMAL LIFE
   FOR 24 HOURS

5. GO TO STEP 1

6. END

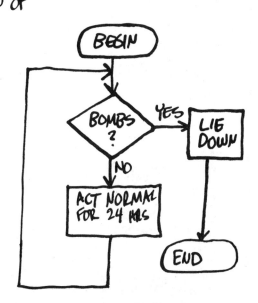

YOU MAY FIND THE FLOW CHART
EASIER TO GRASP THAN THE
WRITTEN "PROGRAM." NOTE THAT
IT MAY CONTINUE INDEFINITELY!!

199

FLOW CHARTS ARE USEFUL IN HELPING TO DESIGN ALGORITHMS — SIMPLE ONES, ANYWAY — AND DESIGNING ALGORITHMS IS WHAT COMPUTER PROGRAMMING IS ALL ABOUT !!

 THE FIRST STEP IN WRITING ANY PROGRAM IS TO **ANALYZE** THE JOB TO BE DONE, AND SEE HOW TO DO IT ALGORITHMICALLY!

FAILURE TO THINK ALGORITHMICALLY HAS CAUSED MANY SOFTWARE NIGHTMARES !! MOST SOFTWARE DESIGNERS HAVE HORROR STORIES ABOUT CUSTOMERS WHO DIDN'T KNOW **EXACTLY** WHAT THEY WANTED !!

200

LET'S TRY A COUPLE MORE EXAMPLES...
A LITTLE MORE LIKE WHAT A COMPUTER
MIGHT ACTUALLY BE ASKED TO DO...

"ROMMATE RECEIPTS"

TWO ROOMATES, LISA AND SOPHIE, SHARE THEIR MEALS. THEY BOTH SHOP FOR FOOD AND SAVE THEIR RECEIPTS. AT THE END OF THE MONTH, THEY WANT TO KNOW WHO OWES WHOM HOW MUCH.

"MULTIPLE PLUG-INS"

THIS ONE ASKS THE COMPUTER TO EVALUATE THE EXPRESSION

$$x^2 + 2x + 10$$

NOT JUST AT ONE VALUE OF X, BUT FOR MANY VALUES, NAMELY

X = 0, 0.1, 0.2, 0.3, ...AND SO ON... UP TO 2.0.

LET'S MAKE THE FLOW CHARTS.

FOR "ROOMMATE RECEIPTS"
WE REASON LIKE SO:

LET S = SOPHIE'S EXPENSES
L = LISA'S EXPENSES

THEN THE TOTAL EXPENSE IS $S+L$, AND EACH ROOMMATE'S SHARE IS

$$\tfrac{1}{2}(S+L).$$

IF LISA OUTSPENT SOPHIE, SO $L>S$ *, THEN SOPHIE OWES LISA $\tfrac{1}{2}(S+L)-S$, OR

$$\tfrac{1}{2}(L-S).$$

OTHERWISE (WHEN $S \geq L$ *), LISA OWES SOPHIE

$$\tfrac{1}{2}(S-L).$$

THE ALGORITHM'S OUTPUT IS TO TELL US WHO OWES WHOM AND HOW MUCH.

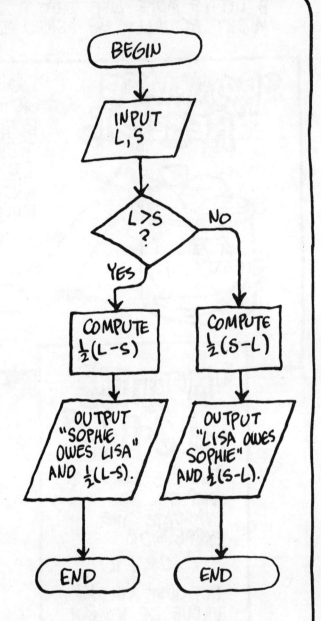

* $>$ MEANS "IS GREATER THAN"; $\geq$ MEANS "IS GREATER THAN OR EQUAL TO";
$<$ MEANS "IS LESS THAN"; $\leq$ MEANS "IS LESS THAN OR EQUAL TO".

IN "MULTIPLE PLUG·INS," WE WANT TO EVALUATE A SINGLE EXPRESSION, $x^2 + 2x + 10$, REPEATEDLY AT DIFFERENT VALUES OF X (NAMELY 0.0, 0.1, 0.2, ... ,1.9, 2.0)

THE CORE OF THE ALGORITHM WILL BE THIS LOOP:

1. PLUG THE CURRENT VALUE OF X INTO $x^2 + 2x + 10$

2. PRINT THE RESULT
3. NEXT X
4. RETURN TO STEP 1.

WE ALSO HAVE TO SPECIFY WHAT X TO START WITH, WHEN TO STOP, AND HOW TO COMPUTE "NEXT X."

NOTE HOW THE FLOW CHART SHOWS HOW THE PROGRAM LOOPS BACK, PLUGGING IN SUCCESSIVE VALUES OF X UNTIL X EXCEEDS 2.

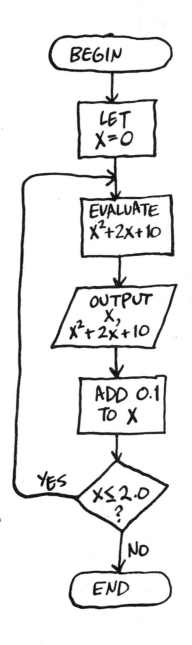

BEGIN

LET X = 0

EVALUATE $x^2 + 2x + 10$

OUTPUT X, $x^2 + 2x + 10$

ADD 0.1 TO X

$X \leq 2.0$?

YES

NO

END

NOW THE $738 QUESTION:
($64 AFTER INFLATION):

IN OTHER WORDS, HOW DO YOU PROGRAM A COMPUTER?

AT THE VERY BEGINNING, PROGRAMMERS WROTE DIRECTLY IN "MACHINE LANGUAGE" — BINARY CODE. THIS WAS OBVIOUSLY A HEADACHE!

SOON THEY SWITCHED TO ASSEMBLY LANGUAGE (SEE P. 174), AIDED BY AUTOMATIC "ASSEMBLERS," WHICH TRANSLATED ASSEMBLY LANGUAGE MNEMONICS INTO MACHINE CODE. STILL SOMETHING MORE WAS NEEDED!

AND FINALLY,

```
┌─────────────┐
│ SOURCE CODE │
└─────────────┘
       │
       ▼
┌──────────────┐
│ COMPILER OR  │
│ INTERPRETER  │
└──────────────┘
       │
       ▼
┌─────────────┐
│ OBJECT CODE │
└─────────────┘
```

THE **HIGHER-LEVEL** PROGRAMMING LANGUAGES WERE INVENTED. THESE CONTAIN FAMILIAR ENGLISH-LIKE COMMANDS, SUCH AS "PRINT," "READ," AND "DO," WHICH ARE TRANSLATED INTO MACHINE LANGUAGE BY COMPLEX PROGRAMS CALLED COMPILERS OR INTERPRETERS. HIGHER-LEVEL PROGRAMS ARE SOMETIMES CALLED "SOURCE CODE," AND THE MACHINE-LANGUAGE TRANSLATION IS CALLED "OBJECT CODE."

THE FIRST HIGHER-LEVEL LANGUAGE WAS **FORTRAN** ("FORMULA TRANSLATOR"), WHICH MADE ITS DEBUT IN THE EARLY 1950'S. SINCE THEN, LITERALLY HUNDREDS OF LANGUAGES HAVE BEEN WRITTEN, EACH WITH ITS OWN ARMY OF RABID DEVOTEES!

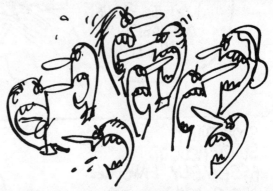

WE'RE GOING TO TAKE A QUICK LOOK AT **BASIC** — **B**EGINNER'S **A**LL-PURPOSE **S**YMBOLIC **I**NSTRUCTION **C**ODE. BASIC IS EASY TO LEARN AND WIDELY USED, DESPITE CRITICISM (ESPECIALLY BY PASCAL ADMIRERS) THAT IT PROMOTES "BAD PROGRAMMING HABITS."

WITH APOLOGIES TO PASCAL, THEN, HERE'S A LITTLE BASIC...

BASIC BASIC

THERE ARE TWO WAYS TO WRITE A BASIC PROGRAM: WITH PENCIL AND PAPER, OR DIRECTLY AT THE COMPUTER.

IT'S GOOD PRACTICE TO PLAN PROGRAMS ON PAPER FIRST, TO WORK OUT THE ESSENTIAL IDEAS AND STRUCTURE, BUT EVENTUALLY YOU MUST SIT DOWN AT THAT KEYBOARD!

PLEASE... BE GENTLE...

SOME MACHINES ARE READY FOR BASIC AS SOON AS YOU TURN THEM ON. OTHERS ONLY BRING IT UP ON COMMAND. IF IN DOUBT, ASK!

WHEN THE COMPUTER IS READY, IT GIVES YOU A "PROMPT" OF SOME KIND: THE WORD "READY" OR JUST THE SIGN ">".

LET'S GET GOING!

THE COMPUTER KEYBOARD RESEMBLES A STANDARD TYPE-WRITER'S "QWERTY" KEYBOARD... EXCEPT THAT AS YOU TYPE, CHARACTERS APPEAR ON THE CRT (CATHODE RAY TUBE) SCREEN, INSTEAD OF ON PAPER. TO GO TO THE NEXT LINE, HIT THE **RETURN** ($\swarrow$) KEY. HERE'S A SIMPLE BASIC PROGRAM:

```
10 REM BASIC MULTIPLICATION
20 READ A, B
30 DATA 5.6, 1.1
40 LET C = A * B
50 PRINT "THE PRODUCT IS"; C
60 END
```

BASIC MATH:

$A+B$ } AS USUAL
$A-B$

$A*B$... A TIMES B
A/B... A DIVIDED BY B

$A \uparrow B$... A TO THE BTH POWER

THE PROGRAM IS NOW STORED IN MEMORY. TO RUN IT, TYPE "RUN", FOLLOWED BY THE RETURN KEY. THE SCREEN DISPLAYS:

```
RUN
THE PRODUCT IS 6.16
```

208

A FEW POINTS TO NOTE:

> EVERY LINE BEGINS WITH A **LINE NUMBER** (10, 20, ...). EVERY LINE OF A BASIC PROGRAM MUST HAVE A NUMBER! IT'S WISE TO COUNT BY TENS, SO YOU CAN INSERT LINES LATER.

> THE FIRST LINE (10) IS A **REMARK**. REMARKS EXPLAIN THE PROGRAM BUT AREN'T EXECUTED BY THE COMPUTER. THE PREFIX "REM" IDENTIFIES REMARKS. WE MIGHT INSERT ONE HERE:

```
20 READ A, B
25 REM THESE ARE THE #S TO BE MULT'D
30 DATA 5.6, 1.1
```

> PROGRAM **STATEMENTS** CONSIST OF **INSTRUCTIONS** ("LET", ETC), **NUMBERS** (5.6, 1.1), **VARIABLES** (A, B, C), **TEXT** ("THE PRODUCT IS"), AND **PUNCTUATION**.

```
50 PRINT "THE PRODUCT IS"; C
```
QUOTES   SPACES   SEMICOLON

> EACH OF THESE HAS A PRECISE MEANING!

NUMERICAL VARIABLES

THINK OF A VARIABLE AS A LABELED BOX IN MEMORY!

A NUMERICAL VARIABLE IN BASIC IS LIKE A VARIABLE IN ALGEBRA. IT ASSUMES A NUMERICAL VALUE, WHICH MAY VARY (BUT IT HAS ONLY ONE VALUE AT A TIME!). ONLY THESE SYMBOLS CAN BE USED AS VARIABLES:

$A, B, C, D, \ldots \qquad \ldots Z$
$A0, B0, \ldots \quad \text{AND} \quad \ldots Z0$
$A1, B1, \ldots \quad \text{EVERYTHING} \quad \ldots Z1$
$\vdots \qquad \qquad \text{IN} \qquad \vdots$
$\qquad \qquad \text{BETWEEN!}$
$A9, B9, \ldots \qquad \ldots Z9$

THERE ARE SEVERAL WAYS TO ASSIGN A VALUE TO A VARIABLE: ONE IS THE **READ - DATA** STATEMENT:

```
20 READ A,B
30 DATA 5.6, 1.1
```

COMMAS ARE ESSENTIAL!!

THIS INSTRUCTS THE COMPUTER TO ASSIGN THE NUMERICAL VALUES IN THE **DATA** STATEMENT — IN ORDER — TO THE VARIABLES IN THE **READ** STATEMENT.

```
20 READ A, B, C
30 DATA 5.6, 1.1
```

THIS IS A **BUG!**

DISGUSTING!

ANOTHER WAY TO ASSIGN VALUES TO VARIABLES IS WITH

LET.

```
10 LET  Q = 6.5
20 LET  R = 2*Q
30 LET  S = Q↑2 + R + 10
```

MAKES R = 13

MAKES S = $(6.5)^2 + 13 + 10$ = 65.25

THE LET STATEMENT ASSIGNS THE VALUE ON THE **RIGHT** OF THE EQUALITY SIGN, "=", TO THE VARIABLE ON THE **LEFT**. THE RIGHT-HAND SIDE MAY BE A NUMBER, OR SOME MATHEMATICAL EXPRESSION INVOLVING OTHER VARIABLES — AS LONG AS THEY ALREADY HAVE VALUES!!

```
10 LET Q = 6.5
20 LET Q = 0.5*R
30 LET S = Q↑2 + R + 10
```

HERE STATEMENT 20 DOES NOT ASSIGN ANY VALUE TO R, BECAUSE R IS NOT ON THE LEFT SIDE OF "=". IN FACT, IF R HASN'T BEEN ASSIGNED SOME VALUE EARLIER IN THE PROGRAM, THEN STATEMENT 20 GIVES Q AN INDETERMINATE VALUE! BUT—

```
10  LET M = 0
20  LET M = M+1
30  LET M = M+1
```

MAKES M = 1

MAKES M = 2

THESE STRANGE-LOOKING STATEMENTS ARE PEFECTLY O.K! "LET M = M+1" MEANS "ASSIGN TO THE VARIABLE M A VALUE EQUAL TO ITS CURRENT VALUE PLUS 1."

PRINT

THIS IS AN OUTPUT COMMAND, MEANING "DISPLAY ON THE SCREEN," NOT "PRINT ON PAPER."

WHAT CAN BE PRINTED?

YOU CAN PRINT ANY TEXT:

```
10 PRINT "ANY NUKES TODAY?"
RUN
ANY NUKES TODAY?
```

QUOTATION MARKS ESSENTIAL!

QUOTATION MARKS REMOVED

PRINT A VARIABLE AND YOU GET ITS VALUE:

```
10 LET X = 77001
20 PRINT X
RUN
77001
```

BUT—

```
10 LET X = 77001
20 PRINT "X"
RUN
X
```

QUOTATION MARKS MAKE THE COMPUTER TREAT X AS A TEXT.

PRINT A MATHEMATICAL EXPRESSION AND YOU GET ITS VALUE:

```
10 LET Z = 1.5
20 PRINT Z↑2 + 2*Z + 10
RUN
15.25
```

BECAUSE
$(1.5)^2 + 2 \times 1.5 + 10$
$= 2.25 + 3.0 + 10 = 15.25$

SEMICOLON (;)

A SEMICOLON AFTER A PRINT STATEMENT CAUSES THE *NEXT* PRINT STATEMENT TO DISPLAY ITS OUTPUT ON THE SAME LINE AND DIRECTLY AFTER THE FIRST ONE'S:

```
10 LET A = 1
20 PRINT "INFINITY IS MORE THAN";
30 PRINT A
RUN
INFINITY IS MORE THAN 1
```

IT'S O.K. TO ABBREVIATE THIS:

```
10 LET A = 1
20 PRINT "INFINITY IS MORE THAN"; A
RUN
INFINITY IS MORE THAN 1
```

FOR EXAMPLE, WE COULD REWRITE THE PROGRAM ON P. 208.

```
10 REM BASIC MULTIPLICATION
20 READ A, B
30 DATA 5.6, 1.1
40 LET C = A*B
50 PRINT "THE PRODUCT OF "; A; "AND"; B; "IS"; C; "."
60 END
RUN
THE PRODUCT OF 5.6 AND 1.1 IS 6.16.
```

THERE ARE ALSO SOME NIFTY TRICKS USING THE **COMMA** AND PRINT, BUT WE WON'T GET INTO IT...

INPUT

IT MAKES THE PROGRAM INTERACTIVE!

THIS STATEMENT ALLOWS THE USER TO ASSIGN VALUES TO VARIABLES WHILE THE PROGRAM IS RUNNING.

THE FORM OF THE STATEMENT:

```
INPUT A
```

WHEN THE PROGRAM RUNS AND REACHES AN INPUT STATEMENT, THE SCREEN DISPLAYS:

```
?
```

THIS INDICATES THAT THE PROGRAM HAS HALTED, AWAITING INPUT. YOU TYPE SOME NUMBER (FOLLOWED BY "RETURN," AS ALWAYS!):

```
5.6
```

AND THE PROGRAM CONTINUES RUNNING.
"INPUT" AND "PRINT" CAN BE USED IN COMBINATION TO LET YOU KNOW WHAT SORT OF INPUT IS EXPECTED:

```
10 BASIC DIVISION
20 PRINT "TYPE THE NUMERATOR."
30 INPUT N
40 PRINT "TYPE THE NON-ZERO DENOMINATOR."
50 INPUT D
60 PRINT N; "/"; D; "="; N/D
70 END

RUN
TYPE THE NUMERATOR.
?  5
TYPE THE NON-ZERO DENOMINATOR.
?  8
5/8 = 0.625
```

TYPED BY THE USER.

 THIS IS THE UNCONDITIONAL BRANCHING INSTRUCTION.

"GO TO (LINE NUMBER)" TRANSFERS CONTROL TO A LINE OTHER THAN THE NEXT. THE PROGRAM THEN CONTINUES FROM THERE, AS IN THIS ENDLESS LOOP:

```
10 LET A=0
20 PRINT A
30 LET A=A+1
40 GO TO 20
```

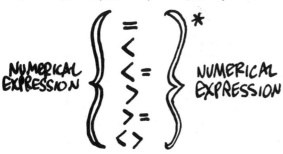 IS THE "SMART," CONDITIONAL JUMP.

IT HAS THE GENERAL FORM
IF (CONDITION) **THEN** (LINE NUMBER).
THE CONDITION HAS THE FORM:

NUMERICAL EXPRESSION $\begin{cases} = \\ < \\ <= \\ > \\ >= \\ <> \end{cases}$ * NUMERICAL EXPRESSION

AS IN | IF A<=B THEN 30 |

THIS ALWAYS INCLUDES THE UNSTATED INSTRUCTION, "OTHERWISE. GO TO THE NEXT LINE."

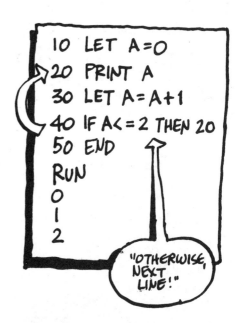

```
10  LET A=0
20  PRINT A
30  LET A=A+1
40  IF A<=2 THEN 20
50  END
RUN
0
1
2
```

"OTHERWISE, NEXT LINE!"

* < LESS THAN, <= LESS THAN OR EQUAL TO, > GREATER THAN, >= GREATER THAN OR EQUAL TO, <> DOES NOT EQUAL.

THIS IS ENOUGH TO WRITE BASIC PROGRAMS FOR THE TWO
ALGORITHMS FROM P. 201:

ROOMMATE RECEIPTS

THE FLOW CHART:

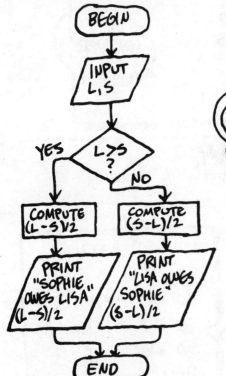

THE PROGRAM:

```
10 PRINT "LISA SPENT"
20 INPUT L
30 PRINT "SOPHIE SPENT"
40 INPUT S
50 IF L>S THEN 80
60 PRINT "LISA OWES SOPHIE"; (S-L)/2
70 GO TO 90
80 PRINT "SOPHIE OWES LISA"; (L-S)/2
90 END
```

SEE HOW "IF-THEN" AND "GO TO" ARE
USED? IF L>S, THEN LINES 60
AND 70 ARE NOT EXECUTED.
OTHERWISE, THEY ARE EXECUTED, AND
LINE 70 ENSURES THAT LINE 80 IS
SKIPPED.

IF THE PROGRAM IS RUN:

```
RUN
LISA SPENT
? 93.75
SOPHIE SPENT
? 77.38
SOPHIE OWES LISA 8.185
```

MULTIPLE PLUG-INS

THE FLOW CHART:

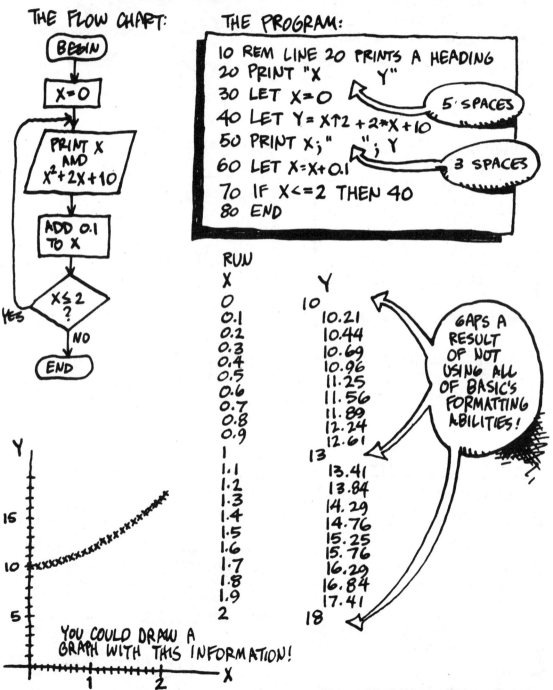

```
BEGIN
X=0
PRINT X AND X² + 2X + 10
ADD 0.1 TO X
X ≤ 2 ?   YES
NO
END
```

THE PROGRAM:

```
10 REM LINE 20 PRINTS A HEADING
20 PRINT "X          Y"
30 LET X=0
40 LET Y= X↑2 + 2*X + 10
50 PRINT X;"      ";Y
60 LET X=X+0.1
70 IF X<=2 THEN 40
80 END
```

5 SPACES

3 SPACES

```
RUN
X          Y
0         10
0.1        10.21
0.2        10.44
0.3        10.69
0.4        10.96
0.5        11.25
0.6        11.56
0.7        11.89
0.8        12.24
0.9        12.61
1         13
1.1        13.41
1.2        13.84
1.3        14.29
1.4        14.76
1.5        15.25
1.6        15.76
1.7        16.29
1.8        16.84
1.9        17.41
2         18
```

GAPS A RESULT OF NOT USING ALL OF BASIC'S FORMATTING ABILITIES!

YOU COULD DRAW A GRAPH WITH THIS INFORMATION!

217

THE "MULTIPLE PLUG-INS"
LOOP IS SO TYPICAL
THAT ALL PROGRAMMING
LANGUAGES HAVE
SPECIAL COMMANDS JUST
FOR SUCH REPETITIONS.
IN BASIC, IT'S ⟹

FOR NEXT

THIS REPLACES THESE
THREE LINES:

```
30 LET X=0
  .
  .
60 LET X=X+0.1
70 IF X<=2 THEN 30
  .
```

WITH THESE
TWO:

```
30 FOR X=0 TO 2  STEP 0.1
  .
  .
60 NEXT X
  .
```

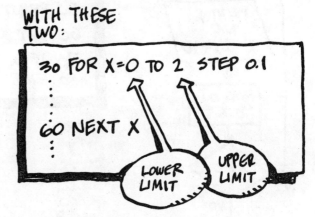

LOWER LIMIT

UPPER LIMIT

THE STATEMENT INITIALLY SETS THE VARIABLE EQUAL TO THE
LOWER LIMIT, EXECUTES THE LINES UP TO "NEXT," INCREMENTS
THE VARIABLE BY THE AMOUNT "STEP," AND REPEATS THE
LOOP UNTIL THE UPPER LIMIT IS EXCEEDED.

A SIMPLE EXAMPLE:

```
10 FOR I =1 TO 4
20 PRINT I*I
30 NEXT I
40 END
RUN
1
4
9
16
```

OMITTING "STEP"
AUTOMATICALLY
MAKES INCREMENT
=1.

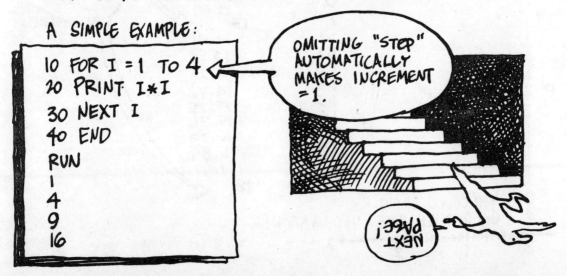

NEXT PAGE!

218

PROBLEMS

PROBLEMS?
WHO HAS
PROBLEMS?

1. WHAT DOES THIS PROGRAM DO?

```
10 INPUT N
20 FOR I=1 TO N
30 PRINT I*I
40 NEXT I
50 END
```

2. REWRITE THE "MULTIPLE PLUG-INS" PROGRAM USING THE "FOR NEXT" STATEMENT.

3. WRITE A PROGRAM WHICH ADDS THE INTEGERS (WHOLE NUMBERS) FROM 1 TO 1,000,000.
DITTO FROM 1 TO N, FOR ANY N.

4. IN THE FIBONACCI SEQUENCE 0, 1, 1, 2, 3, 5, 8, 13, 21, 34,...
EACH NUMBER IS THE SUM OF THE PREVIOUS TWO NUMBERS. WRITE A PROGRAM WHICH GENERATES THIS SEQUENCE.

5. READ ENOUGH OF A BASIC TEXTBOOK TO WRITE A "ROOMMATE RECEIPTS" PROGRAM FOR ANY NUMBER OF ROOMMATES.

THERE ARE PLENTY OF OTHER BASIC FEATURES, ENOUGH TO FILL ENTIRE BOOKS — AND IN FACT TONS OF BOOKS ON BASIC HAVE BEEN PUBLISHED.

BASIC BUILDS BICEPS!

SO... IF YOU'RE INTERESTED IN DISCOVERING STRING VARIABLES, SUBROUTINES, FUNCTIONS, ARRAYS, NESTED LOOPS, HOW TO DEAL WITH DISKS AND AVOID BUGS, ETC ETC ETC, THEN GO TO YOUR LOCAL LIBRARY OR BOOKSTORE AND GET STARTED !!

AND OTHERWISE?

I'M SORAY... THAT POSSIBILITY IS AGAINST UNIVERSITY POLICY...

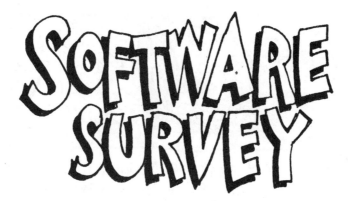

SOFTWARE SURVEY

HERE'S A LOOK AT SEVERAL IMPORTANT AREAS OF SOFTWARE WHICH HAVE EMERGED IN THE YEARS SINCE *ENIAC*...

SYSTEMS SOFTWARE

PROGRAMS ARE
COMMONLY DIVIDED
INTO SYSTEMS SOFTWARE
AND APPLICATIONS
SOFTWARE.

WITH
SOME GRAY
AREA OF
OVERLAP!

APPLICATIONS SOFTWARE DOES "REAL WORLD" JOBS, WHILE
SYSTEMS SOFTWARE EXISTS PURELY TO REGULATE THE
COMPUTER SYSTEM ITSELF.

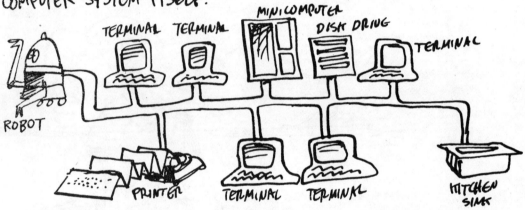

A SYSTEM TYPICALLY
CONSISTS OF ONE OR
MORE INPUT/OUTPUT
DEVICES (TERMINALS,
PRINTERS, CARD READERS,
COMMUNICATIONS PORTS),
PROCESSORS, MEMORY
UNITS (MAIN AND MASS),
AND WHO KNOWS
WHAT ELSE.
SOMETHING HAS TO
COORDINATE IT ALL!

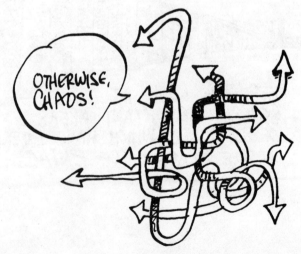

OTHERWISE,
CHAOS!

222

THE PROGRAM THAT DOES IT IS CALLED THE

OPERATING SYSTEM.

IF YOU THINK OF THE COMPUTER'S CORE AS A GIANT ELECTRONIC FILING CABINET (WITH A CALCULATOR ATTACHED), THEN THE OPERATING SYSTEM

☆ CREATES THE STRUCTURE OF THE FILES

☆ MANAGES MEMORY SO THAT DIFFERENT FILES DON'T BUMP INTO EACH OTHER

☆ REGULATES ACCESS TO THE FILES AND THE MOVEMENT OF INFORMATION TO AND FROM OTHER PARTS OF THE SYSTEM...

ETC!

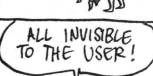

NEXT!

BESIDES THE OPERATING SYSTEM, SYSTEM SOFTWARE INCLUDES OTHER PROGRAMS "IN THE SYSTEM," SUCH AS LOADERS (WHICH LOAD PROGRAMS INTO MEMORY) AND COMPILERS (WHICH TRANSLATE HIGHER-LEVEL LANGUAGE INTO MACHINE CODE).

ALL INVISIBLE TO THE USER!

DATA BASE MANAGEMENT

THIS IS A BIGGIE!

A **DATA BASE** IS JUST A BIG PILE OF INFORMATION: A LIBRARY'S CARD CATALOG, A BANK'S TRANSACTION RECORDS AND ACCOUNT BALANCES, AN AIRLINE'S FLIGHT SCHEDULES AND RESERVATIONS, POLICE FILES, STOCK EXCHANGE DATA — ALL ARE DATA BASES.

A DATA BASE MANAGEMENT PROGRAM ORGANIZES, UPDATES, AND PROVIDES ACCESS TO THE DATA BASE.

IN THE CASE OF AN AIRLINE, FOR EXAMPLE, THE COMPUTER HAS TO BOOK RESERVATIONS, ASSIGN SEATS, ERASE RESERVATIONS WHEN THE CUSTOMER CANCELS, MAKE REASSIGNMENTS IF A FLIGHT IS CANCELED, PRINT THE TICKETS, AND PROVIDE ALL THE FLIGHT INFORMATION TO TRAVEL AGENTS — WORLDWIDE!!

THERE SEEMS TO BE A SLIGHT BUG IN THE OVERBOOKING ALGORITHM...

WORD PROCESSING

WORD PROCESSING SOFTWARE ALLOWS YOU TO WRITE, EDIT, AND FORMAT TEXT — ALL FROM THE SAME KEYBOARD. YOU CAN GO FROM FIRST TO FINAL DRAFT ELECTRONICALLY, BEFORE EVER PRINTING A WORD.

THERE ARE ALSO PROGRAMS TO CORRECT SPELLING — AND EVEN TO FIX SYNTAX AND GRAMMAR. SOON ILLITERATES WILL BE CREATING MASTERPIECES!

A SMALL COMPUTER WITH WORD PROCESSING CAN BE QUITE INEXPENSIVE... THE CATCH IS THAT A "LETTER QUALITY" PRINTER CAN COST TEN TIMES THE PRICE OF A TYPEWRITER!

225

SCIENCE

SCIENCE DEPENDS ON MATHEMATICS, AND COMPUTERS ARE SUPER MATH MACHINES. THE FASTEST, MOST POWERFUL COMPUTERS ARE MAINLY APPLIED TO SCIENTIFIC PROBLEMS.

CRAY-1 COMPUTER, CAPABLE OF 100 MILLION OPERATIONS PER SECOND !!

THESE "SUPERCOMPUTERS" EXCEL AT **SIMULATION**. THE IDEA BEHIND SIMULATION IS TO FEED THE COMPUTER THE EQUATIONS GOVERNING A PHYSICAL SYSTEM AND THEN MATHEMATICALLY "MOVE" THE SYSTEM ACCORDING TO THOSE LAWS.

TAKE SPACE TRAVEL: A COMPUTER CAN GUIDE A CRAFT TO THE MOON, BECAUSE IT CAN INTERNALLY SIMULATE THE ENTIRE FLIGHT !!

COMPUTERS CAN SIMULATE:

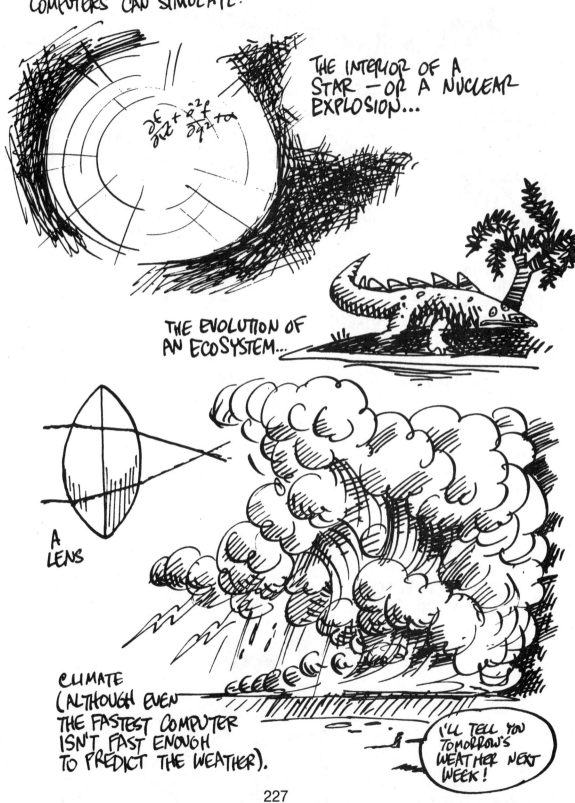

$$\frac{\partial \xi}{\partial t} + \frac{\partial^2 f}{\partial y^2} + \alpha$$

THE INTERIOR OF A STAR — OR A NUCLEAR EXPLOSION...

THE EVOLUTION OF AN ECOSYSTEM...

A LENS

CLIMATE (ALTHOUGH EVEN THE FASTEST COMPUTER ISN'T FAST ENOUGH TO PREDICT THE WEATHER).

I'LL TELL YOU TOMORROW'S WEATHER NEXT WEEK!

GRAPHICS

FROM THE SIMPLEST "PONG" SCREEN TO THE MOST SOPHISTICATED FLIGHT SIMULATOR, THE IDEA IS THE SAME:

DIVIDE THE SCREEN AREA INTO A LARGE NUMBER OF TINY RECTANGLES ("PIXELS") AND ASSIGN EACH ONE A COLOR AND BRIGHTNESS.

THAT'S WHY COMPUTER PICTURES HAVE CORNERS!

BUT THERE ARE ALSO ALGORITHMS FOR SMOOTHING CORNERS!

UNFORTUNATELY, IT TAKES A LOT OF COMPUTER POWER TO DO FANCY GRAPHICS. SMALL COMPUTERS MOSTLY DO THINGS LIKE MAKE PIE CHARTS...

IF ONLY THEY COULD MAKE REAL PIES...

THEN I'D BE IMPRESSED!

228

COMMUNICATION

THE BIGGEST COMPUTER SYSTEM OUTSIDE GOVERNMENT BELONGS TO THE **TELEPHONE COMPANY.**

A VOICE (OR ANY OTHER SIGNAL) CAN BE DIGITALLY ENCODED, TRANSMITTED, AND DECODED.

0010001110101

COMPUTERS ALSO CONTROL THE ROUTING AND SWITCHING OF CALLS THROUGH THE NETWORK — AND KEEP TRACK OF EVERYONE'S BILL!

ANY HUMANS LEFT IN THERE?

COMPUTERS CAN BE PROGRAMMED TO RECOGNIZE PARTICULAR WORDS OR GROUPS OF WORDS — A CAPABILITY NOT LOST ON THE INTELLIGENCE COMMUNITY..

WE CAN AUTOMATICALLY RECORD ANY CONVERSATION CONTAINING WORDS I CAN'T SAY BECAUSE I DON'T WANT TO BE RECORDED...

ARTIFICIAL INTELLIGENCE

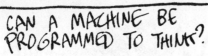

DESPITE THEIR INCREDIBLE SPEED AND ACCURACY, COMPUTERS ARE LOUSY AT PATTERN RECOGNITION, ANALYSIS, HUNCH-PLAYING, AND UNDERSTANDING HUMAN LANGUAGE!

CAN A MACHINE BE PROGRAMMED TO THINK?

ER... WELL... UM... AH... LET ME SEE...

ACTUALLY, WE KNOW VERY LITTLE ABOUT HOW THINKING WORKS... .

SO A BETTER QUESTION IS: HOW CAN YOU TELL IF A MACHINE IS THINKING?

ALAN TURING SUGGESTED THIS TEST: SUPPOSE YOU COULD COMMUNICATE WITH SOMETHING, OR SOMEONE, CONCEALED FROM VIEW. IF, ON THE BASIS OF THE CONVERSATION, YOU COULDN'T SAY WHETHER IT WAS MACHINE OR HUMAN, YOU WOULD HAVE TO SAY IT WAS THINKING!

IT'S A MACHINE!

YEAH, WELL... I HAVE MY DOUBTS ABOUT YOU, JACK!

I PERSONALLY DISLIKE THIS CRITERION, ON THE GROUNDS THAT A SIMULATION ISN'T THE REAL THING...

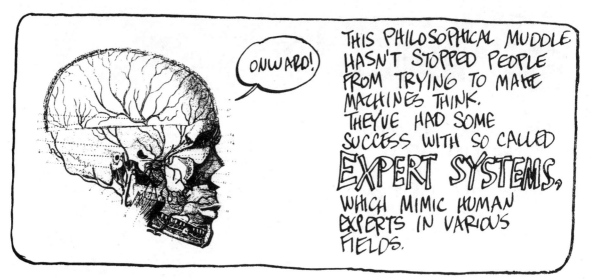

ONWARD!

THIS PHILOSOPHICAL MUDDLE HASN'T STOPPED PEOPLE FROM TRYING TO MAKE MACHINES THINK. THEY'VE HAD SOME SUCCESS WITH SO CALLED **EXPERT SYSTEMS,** WHICH MIMIC HUMAN EXPERTS IN VARIOUS FIELDS.

HOW DO YOU CREATE AN EXPERT SYSTEM? FIRST, INTERVIEW A BUNCH OF EXPERTS — GEOLOGISTS, FOR EXAMPLE — AND FORCE THEM TO SPELL OUT THE ALGORITHMS BEHIND THEIR SKILLS, HUNCHES AND BRAINSTORMS.

THEN LOAD THE COMPUTER'S MEMORY WITH THE HUMANS' KNOWLEDGE BASE... AND THE RESULT IS (SOMETIMES) A PROGRAM WHICH CAN OUTPERFORM ANY HUMAN!!

IF WE'RE SO SMART, WHY DID WE LET THIS HAPPEN?

CRYPT-O-GRAPHY

SHHH!

THERE ARE STANDARD CODES LIKE ASCII (P. 128) FOR CONVERTING WRITTEN TEXT INTO BINARY... BUT WHAT ABOUT USING COMPUTERS FOR **SECRET** CODES??

SECRET CODES USED TO BE STRICTLY MILITARY AND SPY STUFF, BUT NOW MORE AND MORE SENSITIVE INFORMATION IS STORED IN COMPUTER SYSTEMS:

MEDICAL RECORDS, BANK RECORDS, CENSUS DATA, INCOME TAX RECORDS, GRADE TRANSCRIPTS, CORPORATE MEMOS, ETC ETC ETC

 SCRAMBLING DATA HAS BECOME AN IMPORTANT WAY OF PROTECTING PRIVACY !!

ORDINARILY, INFORMATION IS STORED AS A BINARY STRING ANY COMPUTER CAN READ: THE **PLAINTEXT**, IN CRYPTOGRAPHIC JARGON. TO ENCRYPT IT YOU APPLY SOME ALGORITHM **S**, WHICH CONVERTS IT TO A SCRAMBLED MESSAGE CALLED THE **CYPHERTEXT**.

PLAINTEXT →ˢ→ CYPHERTEXT

THEORETICALLY, IT'S IMPOSSIBLE TO RECONSTRUCT THE PLAINTEXT FROM THE CYPHERTEXT WITHOUT KNOWING SOMETHING ABOUT S ... HOWEVER, A POTENTIAL CODE-BREAKER COULD PUT A COMPUTER TO WORK SEARCHING FOR S.

TO BE SECURE, S HAS TO BE SO COMPLICATED THAT EVEN THE FASTEST COMPUTER WOULD TAKE, SAY, A FEW MILLION YEARS TO FIGURE IT OUT!

RECENTLY, THE NATIONAL BUREAU OF STANDARDS APPROVED A FAMILY OF ALGORITHMS AS A DATA ENCRYPTION STANDARD FOR THE NATION. SEVERAL SCIENTISTS SUSPECT THAT THIS STANDARD IS JUST COMPLEX ENOUGH TO STYMIE ORDINARY COMPUTERS, BUT NOT TOO TOUGH FOR THE **NINE** ACRES OF COMPUTERS OF THE NATIONAL SECURITY AGENCY!

CAD/CAM

COMPUTER-AIDED DESIGN / COMPUTER-AIDED MANUFACTURE

USING A COMBINATION OF SPEEDY CALCULATION AND HIGH-RESOLUTION GRAPHICS, COMPUTERS CAN HELP DESIGN NEARLY ANYTHING — FROM JETS TO LENSES TO TYPE STYLES TO OTHER COMPUTERS.

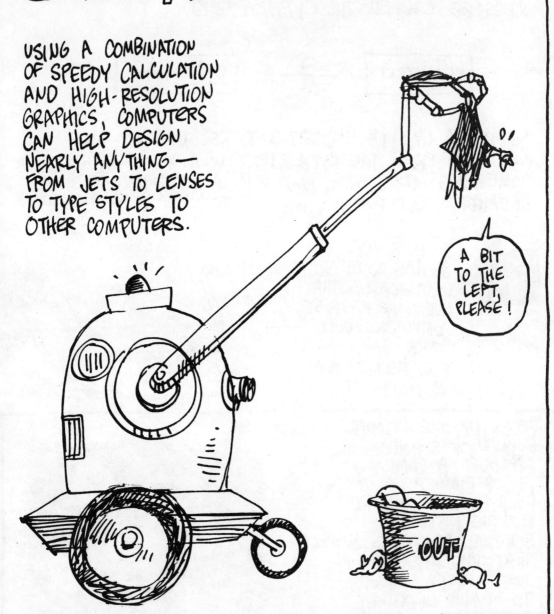

A BIT TO THE LEFT, PLEASE!

OUT

THEN THEY CAN GO ON TO CONTROL AUTOMATIC MANUFACTURING PROCESSES AS WELL. YES, ROBOTS ARE ALREADY HERE!!

WAR

THE MILITARY CAN USE JUST ABOUT EVERY TYPE OF SOFTWARE WE'VE MENTIONED — AND THEN SOME!

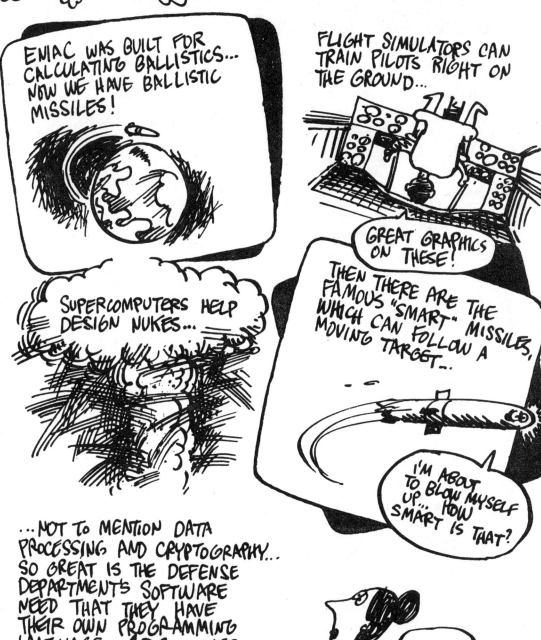

ENIAC WAS BUILT FOR CALCULATING BALLISTICS... NOW WE HAVE BALLISTIC MISSILES!

FLIGHT SIMULATORS CAN TRAIN PILOTS RIGHT ON THE GROUND...

GREAT GRAPHICS ON THESE!

SUPERCOMPUTERS HELP DESIGN NUKES...

THEN THERE ARE THE FAMOUS "SMART" MISSILES, WHICH CAN FOLLOW A MOVING TARGET...

I'M ABOUT TO BLOW MYSELF UP... HOW SMART IS THAT?

...NOT TO MENTION DATA PROCESSING AND CRYPTOGRAPHY... SO GREAT IS THE DEFENSE DEPARTMENT'S SOFTWARE NEED THAT THEY HAVE THEIR OWN PROGRAMMING LANGUAGE: ADA, NAMED AFTER THE UNFORTUNATE LADY LOVELACE.

MERCY!

THIS LITTLE SURVEY ONLY BEGINS TO SUGGEST THE RANGE OF SOFTWARE CURRENTLY AVAILABLE. EVERY DAY THERE'S MORE... SOME PROGRAMS MOVE INTO NEW AREAS, WHILE OTHERS INTEGRATE EXISTING ROUTINES INTO NEW, MORE POWERFUL PACKAGES.

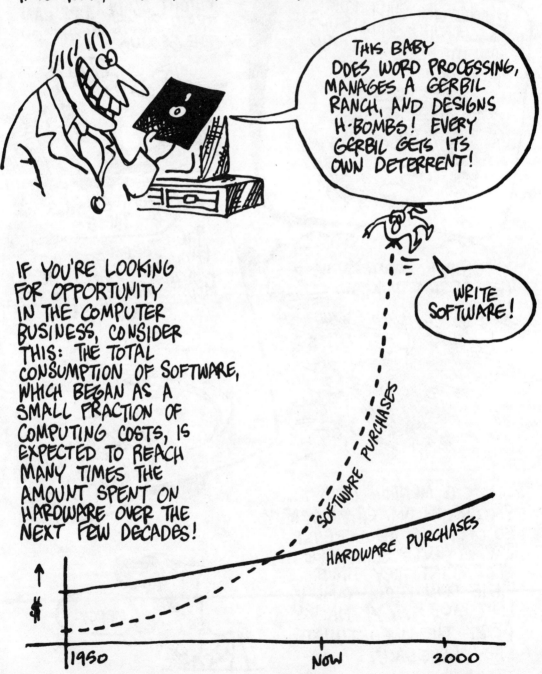

THIS BABY DOES WORD PROCESSING, MANAGES A GERBIL RANCH, AND DESIGNS H-BOMBS! EVERY GERBIL GETS ITS OWN DETERRENT!

WRITE SOFTWARE!

IF YOU'RE LOOKING FOR OPPORTUNITY IN THE COMPUTER BUSINESS, CONSIDER THIS: THE TOTAL CONSUMPTION OF SOFTWARE, WHICH BEGAN AS A SMALL FRACTION OF COMPUTING COSTS, IS EXPECTED TO REACH MANY TIMES THE AMOUNT SPENT ON HARDWARE OVER THE NEXT FEW DECADES!

SOFTWARE PURCHASES

HARDWARE PURCHASES

$

1950   NOW   2000

IN CONCLUSION,

A FEW WORDS ABOUT THIS FAMILIAR SENTENCE:

COMPUTERS ONLY DO WHAT PEOPLE TELL THEM TO DO!

(WHICH IS WHAT COMPUTER SCIENTISTS SAY WHEN THEY WANT TO BE REASSURING...)

TECHNICALLY, IT'S TRUE, IN THE SENSE THAT SOFTWARE CONTROLS COMPUTERS, AND PEOPLE WRITE SOFTWARE...

BUT WHO CONTROLS PEOPLE?!!

FOR EXAMPLE, SUPPOSE A NATION'S STRATEGIC PLANNERS DECIDED TO PROGRAM THEIR COMPUTERS TO ORDER A MISSILE ATTACK AUTOMATICALLY "ON WARNING." CONSIDERING THAT U.S. DEFENSE COMPUTERS SOUND SEVERAL FALSE ALARMS A YEAR, IS THIS REASSURING??

I WAS ONLY FOLLOWING INSTRUCTIONS...

ANOTHER PROBLEM IS THAT ALGORITHMS DON'T ALWAYS DO EXACTLY WHAT THEY ARE SUPPOSED TO.

LARGE SOFTWARE SYSTEMS ARE WRITTEN BY TEAMS OF PROGRAMMERS. LIKE THE ELEPHANT, NO ONE UNDERSTANDS THE WHOLE THING!

COMPUTERS ROUTINELY DO BIZARRE AND UNEXPECTED THINGS, ESPECIALLY WHEN RUNNING NEW, UNTESTED SOFTWARE!

FINALLY, CONSIDER THIS OMINOUS ALGORITHM:

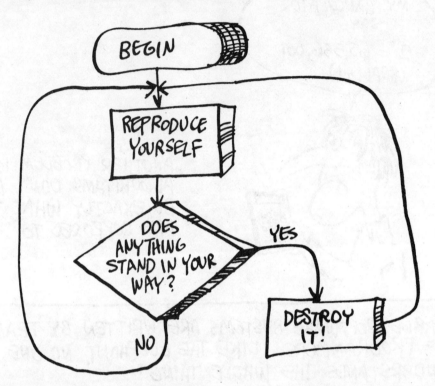

WHILE NO COMPUTER IS INTELLIGENT, MOBILE, OR WELL EQUIPPED ENOUGH —YET— TO EXECUTE THESE INSTRUCTIONS, SUCH A MACHINE REMAINS A THEORETICAL POSSIBILITY. THIS PROGRAM WOULD MAKE IT SOMETHING VERY MUCH LIKE A COMPETING LIFE FORM!!!

AND IF YOU THINK THAT BECAUSE "IT'S ONLY A MACHINE," YOU CAN ALWAYS TURN IT OFF, PONDER THE WORDS OF NORBERT WIENER, A SCIENTIST WHO THOUGHT DEEPLY ABOUT THESE THINGS:

"TO TURN A MACHINE OFF EFFECTIVELY, WE MUST BE IN POSSESSION OF INFORMATION AS TO WHETHER THE DANGER POINT HAS COME. THE MERE FACT THAT WE HAVE MADE THE MACHINE DOES NOT GUARANTEE THAT WE SHALL HAVE THE PROPER INFORMATION TO DO THIS.... THE VERY SPEED OF... MODERN DIGITAL MACHINES STANDS IN THE WAY OF OUR ABILITY TO PERCEIVE AND THINK THROUGH THE THE INDICATIONS OF DANGER." *

* CYBERNETICS, SECOND EDITION, P. 175

SO WELCOME TO THE INFORMATION AGE, AND HAPPY COMPUTING !!

SOME FURTHER READING:

MEDIEVAL AND EARLY MODERN SCIENCE BY A.C. CROMBIE. TELLS HOW ISLAMIC SCIENCE CAME TO EUROPE.

THE MAKING OF THE MICRO BY C. EVANS. NICE DIAGRAMS OF OLD ADDING MACHINES

HISTORY OF MATHEMATICS BY A. GITTLEMAN. DON'T MISS THE STORY OF NAPIER'S "PSYCHIC" CHICKEN!

THE COMPUTER FROM PASCAL TO VON NEUMANN BY H. GOLDSTINE. THE DEFINITIVE ACCOUNT OF ENIAC.

CHARLES BABBAGE, FATHER OF THE COMPUTER BY D. HALACY. AN EASY READ.

CHARLES BABBAGE AND HIS CALCULATING ENGINES, ED. BY P. & E. MORRISSON. IN HIS OWN WORDS!

SYMBOLIC LOGIC AND THE GAME OF LOGIC BY LEWIS CARROLL. MILLIONS OF SILLY SYLLOGISMS

THE MATHEMATICAL THEORY OF COMMUNICATION BY C. SHANNON. CONTAINS TWO PARTS, ONE WITH AND ONE WITHOUT MATH

CYBERNETICS, 2ND EDITION, BY N. WEINER. THE THEORY OF AUTOMATIC CONTROL

UNDERSTANDING DIGITAL ELECTRONICS, BY D. McWHORTER. BOOLEAN CIRCUITS

UNDERSTANDING DIGITAL COMPUTERS, BY P. MIMS. A PERSONAL FAVORITE, BUT LOOK OUT FOR MISPRINTS!

INTRODUCTION TO MICROCOMPUTERS, BY A. OSBORNE (4 VOLUMES). VERY DETAILED

UNDERSTANDING COMPUTER SCIENCE BY R.S. WALKER. MORE ADVANCED TOPICS

ILLUSTRATING BASIC BY D. ALCOCK. A QUICK COURSE, USING QUASI-CARTOONS

USING BASIC, BY R. DIDDAY & R. PAGE. A GENTLER, BUT WORDIER, APPROACH

PASCAL PRIMER BY D. FOX & M. WAITE. IT HELPS TO KNOW BASIC BEFORE READING THIS

FORTRAN COLORING BOOK BY R. KAUFMAN. WITTY, BORDERING ON CORNY

CP/M PRIMER BY S. MURTHA & M. WAITE. A POPULAR OPERATING SYSTEM EXPLAINED

COMPUTER DICTIONARY FOR EVERYONE BY D. SPENCER. A 190-PAGE GLOSSARY IN SEARCH OF A BOOK!

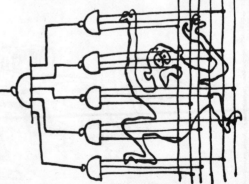

INDEX

ABOUT THE AUTHOR:

LARRY GONICK, THE OVEREDUCATED CARTOONIST, HOLDS TWO DEGREES IN MATHEMATICS FROM HARVARD. HE HAS WORKED AS A *FORTRAN* PROGRAMMER, AND SOME OF HIS BEST FRIENDS ARE IN THE COMPUTER BUSINESS. HE LIVES IN SAN FRANCISCO WITH HIS WIFE AND DAUGHTER, WHO WOULD LIKE TO FIND SOME CARTOON PROCESSING SOFTWARE TO IMPROVE HIS PRODUCTIVITY.